Behind the Badge

True stories of cops being cops

Ron Cowart

Published by Knightyme Productions
www.KnightymeProductions.com

Table of Contents

Introduction

The stories, presented here, in *Behind the Badge*, have been told and retold, so many times, by so many different folks, that they have virtually taken on a life of their own. *Legends* have been created as a result of some of these stories or a combination thereof.

Based on the fact that the author served his entire 33-year law enforcement career in East Baton Rouge Parish, Louisiana, that's where these stories originate from. In all cases the names have been changed to protect the guilty.

After regaling a setting of friends with one or more of the stories collected here, I'm often asked *"is that true; did it really happen?"* And that's a fair question, one which I will answer in this fashion.

At one time, <u>all</u> of the stories in this book were *true*. At least, a portion of it anyway. By that I mean, when the initial story was born, fresh from having taken place, it was served with very little "garnishment" (rarely with no garnishment at all). As the story got passed from one storyteller to another, the "chef" at the time would serve it with his/her own choice(s) of embellishments. In other words, just like any story that has merited being retold, for centuries.

Therefore, to get back to answering the question *"is that true; did it really happen?"* the answer is yes and no! The foundation of all of these stories existed, somewhere at some time. It will be up to you to dissect that which you feel is *creative license* and the cold-hard truth. Just remember one thing that is shared by cops, the world over, when they are sharing one of these gems with a captivated audience.

You simply can't make this stuff up. I hope you enjoy.

1 | The Runaway...Unit

It was a clear day, as the Officers dispersed from Broadmoor Precinct following roll-call. Some were headed to their units, while others were still in the process of off-loading their personal vehicles (prior to take-home units) into their assigned ride for the day.

Normally, this would be like any other day in Broadmoor, in the early 1980's, typically slow, at times, almost boring. However, I did say *normally*.

There was one, young rookie, who had just been "cut loose" by her FTO (Field Training Officer), to begin riding patrol by herself. As was expected, she was excited, perhaps a little anxious. Regardless, she had proven herself to be capable of "riding solo" and this was the big day.

Now, for anyone who may be unfamiliar with the routine, when one is taking over a unit that has just been used for eight previous hours of patrol, by another Officer, it's this. You get in, turn the bar lights (red lights on the roof) on, to make certain they are functioning properly, "tap" the siren once, for the same reason, etc. You're effectively making sure everything is ready and working for your tour of duty.

And that is exactly what the rookie was doing. She had her bar lights on when she looked up and saw the shift Sergeant walking out of the precinct. Thinking of something she needed to ask before she went 10-8 (in service) for her first solo round, she quickly exited her unit and ran to catch him before he got into his unit and drove off. Everything is good...right? Well, not if you accidently left your unit in drive (we drove Chevrolet Malibu's with the 350 4-barrel, at the time), it's not.

She had already reached the Sergeant, when something or someone got her attention. She turned to see her unit heading for the parking lot exit, without her. Just prior to the unit reaching the exit, it made a rather sharp right-angled turn, jumping the curb and neatly leveling the precinct flagpole, flag and all.

Oh, no, that aluminum flagpole failed to stop the runaway unit. It was on a mission! Remember, now, this was day shift, so this is approximately 7:00 am and folks are on the road, headed to work.

The unmanned unit, with its bar lights still turning, dutifully blocked traffic for itself just as it crosses Sharp Road, right in front of what appeared to be an amused gentleman driving a pickup truck. There appears a uniformed *flash*, in the form of a certain rookie, who physically leapt through the open driver's window of the runaway car, just as the latter hits a rather deep ditch on the far side of Sharp Road. The unit plunges and physics, being what physics is demands that this action be met with another action. And so it did.

The rookie's head, now inside the unit, with her lower body still hanging out, proceeds to go against the interior roof of the car, at a pretty good clip. Now, the ditch promptly stopped the car, however, it failed to stop the knot that began to grow, quite noticeably, on the rookies head.

It was reported that the lead driver (in the pickup), who stopped the traffic behind him as he obeyed the unit lights, broke out in applause. Folks, this is one of those stories that tends to "follow" you throughout your career. It's just too good not to.

2 | Ambulance or Hearse?

A fender-bender on Old Hammond Hwy., just west of Sharp Road, in the Spring of 1981 is the setting for this story.

The damage didn't appear all that serious, to either of the two vehicles involved. At the time, however, Old Hammond Hwy. was a two lane road and the area was really just beginning to sprout in business and residential growth, making traffic backup an added concern.

Since one of the drivers was complaining of a back injury, the Officer requested an ambulance (this was just prior to EMS being born in the Baton Rouge area). Now, at the time, there were two privately held ambulance services who serviced the area. Who was called by the dispatcher at the time, depended on who was next in rotation on a list that was managed by Communications personnel.

On this particular call, it was a service that ran out of a local funeral home by the same name, located on North Blvd. This service had been around for a number of years and of course, the fact that the ambulance service part of the business, running out of a funeral home, didn't escape the wit of any cop who experienced their "expertise." This day in 1981 would be no different.

At the time, this ambulance service was still operating Cadillac's version of an ambulance. A rather beefy station-wagon, with a large engine and a single, rotating cherry colored red light on top.

The primary Officer on the scene is all-but-done with writing the accident when the ambulance arrives on the scene. The Officer later reports that he observed three males occupying the lone bench seat of the vehicle, the driver, one riding "shotgun" and one in the middle.

The Officer also stated that he could not see the face of the individual in the middle, as that person was holding a street map, blocking his view. However, the driver was observed clearly mouthing the words "we here" and the map came down.

Then, the driver and "shotgun" exited the wagon and promptly began questioning the wrong "victim." After the Officer got them pointed in the right direction, he noticed that the engine of the ambulance was being revved up, every couple of minutes, by the navigator who was still sitting inside the car.

After this process of revving the engine was repeated a couple more times, the Officer bent down, and through the open driver's window, asked the navigator "why are you doing that?"

The reply was "if I don't, the engine will stop and we won't be able to get it cranked back up."

So, if you felt inclined earlier, to laugh at the idea of an ambulance service being run out of a funeral home, you might note now, there was a certain amount of logic behind the idea.

3 | Jail Trustee & the Body

In the old downtown jail (no longer exists); the one that was on the 4th floor of the old EBR Sheriff's Office (now City Court), there is this story.

In this old jail, there were three isolation cells, more commonly known as "the hole." The holes were primarily used for drunks who found their way in, courtesy of one of the local police agencies, for the purpose of sobering them up before they went on the line, with the general population.

When one of the holes had an "occupant," the shift that was on would check on the individual, hourly (sooner depending on the circumstances), until the person was ready to be moved to the line or bailed out. If the person in the hole was going to be there, when the relieving shift arrived, that shift would then take up the process and so on and so forth.

It was a Saturday, meaning that with the exception of the jail, EBRSO Communications (basement of the same building) and perhaps some stray investigators doing some follow-up in other offices, the overall population of the building were off. The main Sheriff's Office, on the 2nd floor, as was the coffee shop, etc., were closed.

The day shift bevy of Deputies, assigned to the jail, came in to relieve their counterparts on the dog shift. The desk crew (responsible for booking new prisoners in and watching over the holes) were informed "there's one in #2," simply meaning there was an occupant to watch over, in hole #2.

Everything was fine, up until about the second or third hour of the shift. It was at this point that the "desk man" (the Deputy who worked the desk with the shift Sergeant) noticed the new resident had not moved a muscle, while lying on the lone cot in the cell.

Thinking this was a bit curious, he yelled, in an attempt to get the man's attention. No reply.

The Deputy, reporting later, said that he then opened the cell door and walked over to the "sleeping" individual. When he went to nudge him, the Deputy realized that the person was deceased, as rigor-mortis had set in.

The Deputy then dutifully went to his Sergeant and reported his finding. The Sergeant followed his required protocol and finally, the Coroner's Office cleared the way for the hearse to be called in, to transport the deceased. At this point, the reader may like to know that the hearse was dispatched from the same funeral home, from which the ambulance, in the previous story, originated from. The significance of that fact will be better understood, shortly.

Everything has been done, all parties that need-to-know have been informed, etc., so all that is left, is to await the hearse.

Now, before the hearse arrives, it's also important, for the story, to understand that this jail has been around for many years. This story takes place in 1979 and the jail was old then. Meaning, the lone elevator used to access the jail, by everyone, is a *manually operated* elevator. That is, it required a person to ride along and operate the elevator for whoever was arriving or leaving. As such, it was an assignment that fell to a jail "trustee" or inmate, who would receive "good time" or time knocked off his sentence, for operating the elevator on twelve-hour shifts.

The hearse arrives and the trustee transports two suit-clad attendants and their gurney, up to the jail.

As the attendants are being led to the deceased, the trustee responsible for operating the elevator (his "street name" was Kingfish), sashays up to the desk Deputy and tugs on the Deputy's shirt sleeve. The Deputy turns and asks what he needs.

Kingfish replies "uh, Deputy, I don't think I can ride that elevator with a dead man." The Deputy, who is just busy enough to not be in the mood for any games, instructs Kingfish to carry his butt back to the elevator.

Moments later, the same Deputy feels another tug on his

sleeve and again, it's Kingfish, stating his position yet again. This time, the Deputy made it clear. If Kingfish didn't man up and get back to the elevator, there would be <u>two bodies</u> going to the funeral home.

Well, Kingfish understood that and mumbling something about dead bodies and h'ants (haunts), he slowly trudged back to his assigned position.

The funeral home attendants were just emerging from the hole, with the deceased, strapped to the gurney and covered with a sheet. They now head for the elevator.

The Deputy reported that he walked over, with the attendants, to the elevator, just to make certain that Kingfish didn't have any last-second reservations about doing his job. He added that Kingfish pushed his body up against the controls and closed his eyes, while the attendants maneuvered the body-laden gurney in behind him, in the elevator, which wasn't much larger than a telephone booth.

To his credit, Kingfish closed the elevator door and proceeded towards the basement. However, prior to the Deputy getting back to the desk, there was heard what was later described as a blood-curdling scream, originating from the area of the elevator shaft. And since one couldn't simply press a button to call the elevator, the Deputy who had since rushed back to where the elevator would be could only wait. A couple of minutes went by and the elevator was heard to be moving. Seconds later, its door opened at the jail level and to the waiting Deputy.

Based on what the funeral home attendants, who incidentally, along with the deceased, were the only ones present on the elevator, reported to the Deputy, the following took place, just previous to the scream that everyone, within three city blocks had heard.

They said that the elevator had gotten somewhere between the 2nd and 3rd floors, when the deceased, who evidently was not as secure on the gurney as originally thought, came loose. His "dead-weight" led him to fall over and onto the back of Kingfish, the elevator operator, who promptly "screamed like a banshee," stopped the elevator and exited same, like a "scalded dog," running to parts unknown.

The Deputy went in search of the missing trustee and found him in an office, on the second floor, shaking like a leaf on a windy day. He looked at the Deputy and said "I didn't escape but I tole you Deputy, I tole you, it's bad mojo to ride with a dead man."

No additional charges (escape) were filed on Kingfish and he was permitted to retain his position as "elevator operator."

4 | Running of the Roaches

Here's another story from the downtown jail.

As was pointed out in a previous story, the downtown jail was old. There was no air conditioning (except for the Major's office) and it claimed its share and then some, of roaches. Yes, those God-awful little bugs that seem to popup in your path when you least expect it. Only, the roaches that called the downtown jail home were anything but little. They were often referred to as "tanks" (Army tanks).

Now, on the dog shift in the jail, largely depending on what day of the week it was and what the weather looked like, it could get downright boring. Some Deputies would chat while others would read. One, who was attending LSU, would use the time to study.

Others, meanwhile, would find "different" things to do, much like the Deputy who is largely behind this story.

These were the days of "Liquid Paper," the little black-labeled bottle, with the white screw-on cap, that contained "paper" in liquid form. Originally intended to correct mistakes on typewritten documents, one particular Deputy employed the solution for other purposes.

He would use the Liquid Paper (that came with a small brush attached to the inside of the cap), to "paint" numbers on the back of roaches. That way, he could tell if he was seeing the same roach all the time or if there were really that many different ones. Hey, don't blame me, I told you it got boring up there.

Then, on one memorable dog shift evening, a Louisiana State Trooper brought a DWI suspect into the jail. Now, this was one of those good-natured drunks. He wasn't boisterous or combative. He was clowning around with the Trooper and Deputies to boot.

The desk Deputy asked the new resident to empty his pockets and place everything on the counter, as securing personal items before being placed into a cell, was standard operating procedure.

The man reached into his front pants pocket, removing some loose change and keys. As he went to lay the items on the counter-top, a large roach, with the #7, clearly painted in white, on its back, went leisurely by. The DWI cocked his head, watching the roach disappear downrange, turned back to the Deputy and asked "did you see that??"

The Deputy, without batting a lash, replied "see what?"

The drunk, didn't say anything. He commenced emptying his other pants pockets, when old #4 went tooling by. This was over the top for the drunk guy. He looked at the Deputy and said "don't tell me you didn't see that!?!"

"See what?" the Deputy replied.

The DWI simply shook his head vigorously and said "that's it. You won't see my ass up here ever again. When you start seeing roaches with numbers on'em, it's time to lay off the sauce!"

And he was never seen again.

5 | It's a Man!!

One more story from the jail, before we switch gears.

Even though the female population in the downtown jail was significantly smaller than that of the men, there was a wing built specifically for them. And as such, there was a female Deputy, known as a Matron, assigned on each shift, to watch over that population and process in any new arrivals.

Such was the case on one evening shift.

A new arrival, a drop-dead, gorgeous blonde, wearing white leather and silk and having one of those furry looking "snakes" that one throws around their necks, this too being white. Baton Rouge Police had brought her in and one would not be faulted if one were to yell back at the on-duty Matron with "one coming back to you!"

That is, unless you had been around long enough to realize all wasn't as it appeared.

You see, this blonde bombshell, although truly a looker,

was 100% male. His "street name" was *Peaches* and if anyone, anywhere, ever had any doubts that a person was born the wrong gender, Peaches would have, without a doubt, been *exhibit A.*

Now, as luck would have it, Officers from Baton Rouge Police brought Peaches in on the same day that there was a relatively new Matron on duty. The desk Sergeant didn't even hesitate as he yelled "Matron, we got one coming back to you!"

Peaches, who began walking that direction, "threw" the ruffled snake around his neck, turned and looked over his should at the Sergeant and said "you're so baaaaad," all the while grinning from ear-to-ear.

One of the duties of the Matron is to strip search and provide a new arrival with jail clothes, prior to their placing the new arrival on the line.

Roughly five minutes went by and the desk Sergeant heard a scream of exclamation "**it's a man!!**" at which time the new Matron comes flying out towards the desk, followed by a grinning, half-naked Peaches.

In the jail, entertainment was at a premium. One had to find it where one could or create it.

6 | Wrong Way

Once again, we find ourselves on day shift, working out of Broadmoor Precinct, about 1981.

Two Officers were sitting in their separate units, side-by-side, each facing a different direction, with their drivers windows rolled down, and chatting. They were in a shopping center parking lot, located at the corner of Florida Blvd. and Sharp Road, as they watched another Officer from their squad; stop a car on Florida Blvd.

They continued to watch, from their position, as the other Officer issued a citation and then he and the offending driver drove off. The Officer, having spotted the other two, drove to their location.

On arriving, the third Officer exited his unit and, turning sideways, walked between the units to where the other two were talking. He said "I think I just screwed up."

Well, the other two couldn't believe that this one could possibly screw-up, much less admit too it, so they set out to have as much fun with that before one asked, "well, trainee what did you do?"

The reply was "well, I wrote that guy a ticket for going the wrong way on Florida."

Since that didn't seem to be an open and shut case of his having screwed up, clarification was requested.

"Well, after I wrote it and he drove off, I figured out it was me that was going the wrong way on Florida."

It's been said before, you just can't make this stuff up.

7 | The Mannequin Prank

The setting; Carlotta St. (2nd District area) around 1992.

It's evening shift and LSU is full of students, staff, etc. In other words, the area population and therefore the number of calls are significantly up.

A two-man unit gets dispatched to a man down call on Carlotta Street, possible electrocution. Being relatively close, they arrive rather quickly and exit their unit, in a small parking lot. The sun has already set, making it just a little bit of a challenge to see anything clearly.

The first thing Officers note is the presence of soft, albeit audible titter coming from unknown sources, the latter situated in dark recesses off of the perimeter of the parking lot. They look questionably at each other without speaking.

Then, one of the Officers spots what appears to be a man lying prone on the parking lot, across a black colored electrical cable. While at first glance, it would sound like this could be startling, it was also obvious to the Officers that both ends of the cable were in plain view. And neither end was attached to anything remotely considered a power source.

Further investigation revealed that the "victim" was stiff as a board, as he should have been. "He" was a mannequin. Now, for the sake of those who may recall this, he wasn't just any mannequin.

At the time, there was, around Baton Rouge, a series of billboards, advertising a popular, well-known home repair service. Adding to their already realistic billboards, the company had included a mannequin, wearing coveralls, a work shirt, work boots and a cap. The mannequin was in a fixed position, so as to appear that he was working on something that was painted on the billboard. The "dead" mannequin was one of these.

The Officers had to laugh as well, even though the joke was supposed to be on them. However, they successfully turned the joke around, when they drove off with the mannequin straddled across their hood.

Now, the dummy was too stiff and too tall to fit in the back seat, so the Officers rolled their windows down, and with the passenger holding onto the ankles and the driver holding onto the wrists, made their way down Highland Road to 2nd District, with the mannequin directly in front of their windshield. They said it was rather funny, watching oncoming drivers trying to figure out if this was a new way to transport prisoners.

Arriving at 2nd District, the Officers quickly organized a plan, whereas they would rush into the District, one holding the mannequin in a headlock (and beating it in the head at the same time), while the other would have his legs trapped.

Inside the District, the radio room, where the Officer on desk duty for the shift was situated, was a room to itself, the top half of the wall being glass and the bottom half being cinder-blocks. The plan was to rush the mannequin in, while beating it and run it, headfirst into the cinder-block wall (just to make certain the desk Officer wasn't sleeping on duty).

Unknown to the Officers at the time, there was a female Sergeant, sitting on top of an unused desk, in the same radio room, talking to the desk Officer. In fact, she was sitting exactly above the spot where they planned on running the dummy into the wall. The plan, the officers and the mannequin all moved forward.

Yelling, beating, slamming, more yelling, more beating, then kicking, was all followed by a shrill voice screaming "WHAT THE HELL IS GOING ON?!?"

The Officers then realized the words emanated from the wide-eyed Sergeant who later stated that she saw her career flash before her eyes. Everyone, including her, then enjoyed a good, hearty laugh.

That mannequin stayed in the District for several weeks afterwards and was the unerring participant in additional pranks, one of which included it being found in the stall of the women's bathroom at the District.

Do what you can, when you can, 'cause there ain't no telling when things might get serious.

8 | The Tree Monster

It's evening shift, working out of 2nd District, about 1994. Two Officers (who went through the police academy together) are riding in two different units, scouring zone 2-A for corner drug deals, moving violations, anything they can find.

The one in the lead unit turns south from Government St. onto S. 18th, where they spot a canary yellow Volkswagen Bug, headed in the same direction. A violation is noted and the Bug gets lit up and stopped at S. 18th at Cherokee.

All of this takes place in a residential area. There are trees everywhere, you know, the big old Live Oaks, some Maples, all of them really large and really old (for trees). The Officers have the Bug's lone occupant (the driver) step out and to the rear of his car. It takes about three minutes for these seasoned veteran's to recognize that they have a 100% law abiding (save for the one minor violation) stopped and begin the process of "shutting down" to let him go.

All of a sudden, one of the Officers cocks his head and looks up into an overhanging Oak tree. The move is so sudden and unexpected that both the other Officer and the poor soul they stopped look in the same direction.

At this point, the initial Officer calmly and rather quietly asks his partner "do you see it?"

Did I mention these two went through the Academy together? They had one of those unique, on-duty relationships, whereas one knew what the other one was doing or going to do, without a word being exchanged between the two.

The partner, almost in a whisper, replies "yeah, I see it."

Now, the guy these two Officers had stopped, had already made three or four closely spaced circles, without ever taking his eyes from the tree limbs above. He was vainly searching for the "it" that simply did not exist.

The initial Officer suggested, again, very quietly, that they should slowly move towards their units, surmising that the citizen would head for the security of his own car.

Now, follow along carefully here.

Bother Officers reach their units, get in and drive off, eastbound on Cherokee. They then turn north onto Park Blvd. (in the Garden District) and head straight out to Government Street. On reaching Government, they turn west and proceed to S. 18th (the original roadway they stopped the guy on) and then turned south on S. 18th. For those who know this area, they essentially made one very big block, actually encompassing several smaller blocks in the process.

Just prior to reaching Cherokee, where they had pulled the man over, they were astonished to discover that the same guy, was still outside the same canary-yellow bug and still vainly searching for whatever in hell was in those trees!!

The Officers left the area and chatted about it on their CB radios. They couldn't help but wonder what would happen if they guy found *something*!

Both Officers are long retired, with one living out-of-state now. They still enjoy a hearty laugh about *The Tree Monster* when they talk.

9 | Rocket's Red Glare

For many years, the Baton Rouge Police Department had a Rescue Division. When the division was first formed, the primary task of the Officers who manned it, was to operate the Hurst Tool (more commonly known as the *Jaws of Life*), to expedite the extrication of victims from major car accidents and the like. The crew that manned the Rescue Division were not only regular police officers; they were also trained, across the board in many life-saving skills, that the average Officer in Uniform Patrol, of the day, had not learned.

Regardless of the training and regardless of the fact that, in the early days of the division, they operated one of just a handful of Hurst Tools to be found throughout the entire state, they were cops through and through.

In 1984, the Rescue Division had moved from their original location, in a shed behind Baton Rouge Fire Department HQ, located then at Florida and N. 22nd, to the main building of the old Hollywood Elementary School on Amarillo Street, in North Baton Rouge. That's where this story is staged.

To better understand and perhaps enjoy this story, it's

important to understand that the building that was the old Hollywood School, was not air conditioned. In the spring and especially the summer, one could enter the building and see windows open in almost every former classroom (now used as offices) in the entire place. Such was the case of the Rescue Division.

Now, in the old school at the time, there were a variety of Baton Rouge Police offices, besides Rescue. The Burglary Division, Narcotics, Recruiting, the Training Academy, Bicycle Registration, Internal Affairs and perhaps one or two more also called the old building "home." For this story though, we'll stay with Rescue and Internal Affairs.

If you were to stand outside, in front of the old Hollywood School, and face it, you would see a building that had been erected, I believe in the 1930's. It had two "main" entrances," one being on the west end of the main building and the other being on the east end of the main building. The Rescue Division, along with Bicycle Registration occupied all of the former classrooms on the east end of the ground floor.

Just outside of the easternmost wall of the main building, was a separate unattached building (perhaps three feet separation – it's important for the story), which was home to Internal Affairs.

By this time, I suppose it's a "given" that the police

department was well stocked with "characters." I feel it would be somewhat of an understatement to say that, as far as divisions go, Rescue may have had more characters assigned to it than just about any other division of comparable size. Now, you take one of the "characters from Rescue" and develop a "prank competition" (to ascertain who can out prank the other) between him and another character; this one from Internal Affairs and well, you have the foundation for something hilarious taking place almost every day of the week.

Now, just a reminder. No air conditioning in the building, thus the windows are left open frequently. Spring is in the air and things around the Rescue Office can get downright boring, until which time a call comes out. Such was the setting on this beautiful day in 1984. A slow paced day; nothing at all happening and the Lieutenant, who was over Rescue and Bicycle Registration was sitting at his desk.

Okay, well, he was leaned back, in a rickety officer chair, with his feet propped on his desk. Now, in all fairness, he did say he didn't nap at his desk. He would use that time, to do some serious thinking about how to fine-tune the Division. However, it was an honest mistake, as this deep thinking would result in him squinting his eyes to the point of appearing closed. He was not sleeping.

Like I said previously, there was nothing happening on this warm, slow, Spring day. That was about to change.

The stars must have been in just the right alignment, as both pranksters, the one in Rescue and the one in Internal Affairs, were both at their respective offices. And just the day before, the one in Rescue had advanced his score on the one in IA. Whatever had taken place the day before, must have been good, as the character from IA said later, that he planned on his revenge, of and on, all night.

Here is the setting.

Two offices on the east end ground floor of the main building. The first office housing Bicycle Registration and the Lieutenant over both. The second office was where the men reported for work, to pick up their interdepartmental mail, etc. Internal Affairs right next door.

The prankster from IA had, in his possession, for the time, a very large bottle rocket. One that was at least three or four times larger than the standard pffftt/pop variety. He carefully placed "score equalizer" onto his office window sill, aiming it directly for the open window of the second set of offices of Rescue. Having just confirmed, via a confederate, that his "target" was in place and ripe for defeat, he retrieved his cigarette lighter from his desk.

Just prior to lighting the fuse, he carefully eyed the fuselage of the rocket, making certain of it's aim and intended trajectory was unhindered. With what was soon to prove a premature smile of victory on his face, he ignited the fuse.

Anyone that has ever fooled with any bottle rocket, regardless of it's caliber, knows that the only certain way to get it to a specific destination is to fire it through a pipe, the latter long enough to take it within inches of the target or "walk" it there.

There were simply too many variables involved for this particular launch, to get comfortable in advance, with the planned outcome. Not the least of which, was the three-foot wide breezeway, between the two buildings, with the emphasis on *breeze*.

The fuse is lit, the rocket launches and the smile of unadulterated victory disappears as quickly as the rocket does, the latter in the wrong direction.

For reasons nobody can be certain of, the rocket took an immediate left turn upon exiting the IA window sill. It proceeded, rather rapidly, down the squat breezeway and promptly ricocheted off the eave of the building which, just as quickly nudged the projectile into the front Rescue Office.

The rocket, seemingly, at this point, with a mind of its own, then elected to complete its mission within about eighteen inches of the deep-thinking Lieutenant. As was pointed out earlier, this particular rocket was several times larger than the standard "bottle rocket." The ensuing explosion, from all indications, matched the size of the rocket as well.

At this point, you may recall that the chair the Lieutenant was occupying was best described as "rickety." The reason for that description is that the chair surrendered its prone cargo, delivering the studious Lieutenant sharply to the floor, with a very loud and equally unglamorous thud.

There are some, to this day, that believe two things about that particular event.

1. They believed that the Lieutenant's unceremonious impact with the floor was captured on LSU's seismograph. It was not.

2. They believed that the phrase "all hell broke loose" was coined that day in 1984. That, too, is untrue.

What was true however, was that the previously described "competition" ended that day, with Rescue being declared the winner, based on a "misfire."

10 | The Urine Test

This story is also attributed to the Rescue Division. However, it's two Rescue Division Commanders later and Rescue, for this piece, has moved from the old Hollywood School, where it was for the previous story.

The year is 1986 and the location is the old Broadmoor Precinct, on Sharp Road. At this time, now, Broadmoor is known as 5th District and is located on Coursey Blvd. I know. It changed later to 3rd District but for a while it was 5th District.

Anyway, Rescue now has the old precinct building on Sharp. And this particular day in 1986, was a "training day," a day whereas everyone assigned to the division was expected to attend.

One Rescue Officer, just about to leave his house, to head for the office, receives a phone call from another Officer, who was already present at said office. The caller wanted to give the other one a "heads-up" on a prank that one of the illustrious Rescue Sergeant's was playing on everyone who came in.

It seemed that the Sergeant had worked extra-duty the night before, at the Baton Rouge General ER (a long-time security detail) and had gotten his hands on several Pyrex, urine-test cups. When an Officer would arrive for the days training, this same Sergeant was handing them a specimen cup and telling them they had to take a urine test. It seems that nobody was falling for the gag either.

Now, the Officer who received the call from his partner, at home, was enroute to the office. While driving, he was mulling over what he could do, to "even the score" on the upcoming prank about to be played on him.

In 1986, at the corner of Florida Blvd. and McGehee Dr., there was a 7-11 store situated on the southwest quadrant. As the Officer approached the intersection and saw the store, an idea came upon him.

He stopped, went inside the store and purchased one bottle of Barq's Crème Soda.

Upon arriving at the Rescue Office, the Officer bootlegged the bottle of crème soda and entered the office via a side door, out-of-site of the rest of the crew, who were gathered in the roll-call room. He then entered the office bathroom, where he secreted the bottle on the floor, and out-of-sight behind the toilet.

The Officer then emerges and walks into the roll-call

room, where he is immediately contacted by the Sergeant, who is handing him a still-sealed, new urine test cup. The Sergeant tells him that he is the last one to do so but he must provide a urine sample. The Officer looks at the others in general who all either nod or agree. He then shrugs and walks into the bathroom from whence he had just came.

After closing the door, the Officer retrieves the crème soda and fills the specimen jar to the "required fill line." He then walks unceremoniously back into the roll-call room.

At this point, even the Officer who had originally called him was giving him a quizzical look, as he handed the container to the Sergeant. The Sergeant let loose with a belly laugh, saying that HE (the Officer) was the ONLY one to take the bait. He could keep his urine sample as it wasn't truly needed.

The Officer, looking as sheepish as he could muster, inquired "then, you really don't need this?" The Sergeant replied, "heck no, I was just getting some of y'all back for all the gags you pull."

With that, the Officer uncovers the "urine sample" and says, "well, we can't let it go to waste" and gulps the "shot" down, licks his lips and places the jar on the table.

At this point, he has everyone's undivided attention,

especially the Sergeant who had tried to prank him from the start. The Sergeant's eyes were wide when he exclaimed "hell, he's crazier than I am!!" The Officer looked over and saw that his partner, who had called him, was standing there with his mouth open but still with a "hopefully knowing" look on his face.

The "target" Officer laughed and then produced the crème soda bottle, telling the others what he had done. Everyone laughed and pointed at the Sergeant, reminding him that he was not only still behind in the gag department, he was now officially farther behind!

You never knew, in that division, when you would have to respond to a major car accident and use the Jaws of Life to extricate a deceased person or someone's child from the wreckage. You did what you could, when you could, to keep things "light."

11 | 1 Ambulance or 2?

This story originates from about 1981 and the Broadmoor Precinct area. It's day shift and again, things are relatively slow. That's about to change.

An Officer gets dispatched to the Albertson's supermarket, located at Florida Blvd. and Sherwood Forest, relative to a first-aid, woman down inside the store.

As stated previously, it was a somewhat slow day, so there was actually more than one unit responding to the call. Now, for the general gist of this story to be better understood, it's important that the reader knows, that the primary Officer who arrives on the scene, is still relatively new and very much full of piss and vinegar.

In other words, to say that he is anxious to "put his best foot forward" would be putting it mildly. As true as that may have been, it remains in the memory of several, that day was not one that would go down as "putting his best foot forward."

The Officer enters the store, in the very front, where there is a clear break or split, separating the single row of cash registers; one large grouping to the left; one to the right.

Remember, it's day shift and the Officer has entered the store from a bright, sunny day outside, while still wearing his genuine imitation aviator sunglasses.

He looks left and immediately spots an Albertson's manager, who is signaling the Officer that the problem is several cash registers down the way. He takes off at a sprint and when he comes to the register that the manager is standing next too, he looks and clearly sees a woman, in distress, lying in an aisle, some twenty to twenty-five feet away.

The dedicated, mission-focused Officer runs in the direction of the victim.

Do you recall the mention of the fact that the Officer was wearing sunglasses? Well, he still had them on, when he bolted in the direction of aisle 13, on his *white horse*. Unfortunately, his eyes had not yet grown accustomed to the lighting, therefore, he failed to notice one of those yellow-colored plastic chains that are commonly used to signify when a register is closed.

He hit that chain, at almost full gallop, at a level just below his waistline. Others, who witnessed the near-perfect resulting somersault, including the manager, would later rate said flip a "9."

The Officer ended up solidly on his back and looking up

at the ceiling. The face of the manager then appeared over him, with the manager very calmly stating "we have one ambulance on the way for the lady. Would you have me ask for a second one?"

Folks, there was not enough cash in the city coffers to have that Officer ask for help in standing, much less a second ambulance. He stood up, minus his sunglasses, which had gone flying, then sliding down the aisle, and proceeded to the victim, albeit noticeably slower in speed.

Again, there are some events that just seem to follow one through their careers. This was one of those.

12 | Where's Your Hat?

The year is 1983 and the setting is 2nd District, specifically, Zone 2-A, more specifically, atop the "new bridge." For those of you who may not be familiar with the Baton Rouge area, we have two bridges, both of which span the Mississippi River, several miles apart. Based on the virtue that one of the bridges we built before the other, it is referred to, mainly by locals, as the "old bridge." The only thing pertinent to this story is this took place on the "newer span."

An Officer gets dispatched to a "minor 52" (minor fender-bender), westbound, on the apex of this bridge. He arrives and exits his unit and upon confirming there are no injuries, begins the process of "writing the wreck."

A few minutes later, a Corporal (a "real" Corporal who had to take the test, at the time, to make the rank) arrives on the scene, to see if he can assist.

Now, it's important to understand that at this time, throughout the Baton Rouge Police Department, it was required that any and all Officers, regardless of rank, when exiting their unit in an official capacity, would don their uniform "taxi-cab driver" hat (a common description, largely used by those who despised the thing).

It's also important to know that the Officer, at the wreck scene, was wearing his hat. The Corporal, on the other hand, was not.

Less than five minutes after the Corporal had arrived on the scene, an unmarked police unit (Ford LTD) drove up and parked behind the Corporal's unit.

Lo & behold, from the unmarked unit, steps the police department's only (only one served at a time) full-bird Colonel. This was the number 2 man, answering only to the Chief, in the department and he was in full regalia, meaning a dress uniform, complete with coat and most importantly (for this story), his hat, whose brim was adorned with "scrambled eggs," the latter denoting administrative personnel.

Now, the young Officer momentarily forgot where he was, much less what he was doing, as he was trying to juggle an aluminum clipboard and salute, all at the same time. The Colonel, obviously on a mission, walked past the stunned Officer like the latter didn't even exist, and proceeded to the Corporal.

Upon reaching the Corporal (this Corporal, incidentally, had what seemed to be a perpetual grin on his face, a fact which seemed to annoy some others, especially those of higher rank), the Colonel clearly asked "where is your hat Corporal?"

At this exact point-in-time, a rather healthy breeze (remember, we're on the top of the bridge, over the river) develops and promptly removes the Colonels distinguished-looking hat, sending it over the bridge railing and ultimately to parts unknown, several stories below.

Without missing a beat, the aforementioned perpetual grin never leaving his face, the Corporal responds "my hat is in my unit sir, where, may I ask, is yours?"

This Colonel had solid white hair, meaning the ensuing bright red color, which his face turned too, stood out somewhat significantly. He didn't utter one word as he turned and marched back to his unit, entered and drove off.

The Corporal looked at the Officer, boldly grinned and said "he never did answer my question."

Another one of those times one will never forget.

13 | In Hot Water

This story takes place in 1985, at the old Hollywood School building, on Amarillo, mentioned in some previous stories. It also involves the Corporal from our previous *"Where's Your Hat"* story, only it's a couple of years later and he is now a Sergeant.

Sgt. "Perpetual Smile" drives into the rearmost parking lot of the complex and sees an Officer who is busy washing one of the Rescue Units, a Ford Bronco. The Sergeant drives over to the Officer, greets him and says something to the effect "I'm going into the weight room. I'm expecting two ladies to arrive shortly, looking for me. If you don't mind, tell them where I'll be."

Since the Officer was going to be busy outside, cleaning the unit, he was only happy to oblige. Now, before we progress any farther into what will take place, note that the Sergeant was in uniform and in his unit, when he arrived.

Sure enough, not more than ten minutes go by, when a car, containing two rather attractive ladies, pulls up and the passenger window rolls down. The blonde, riding shotgun asks the Officer if he knew where they could find the Sergeant.

As promised, the Officer carefully points and shows them where the Sergeant indicated he would be. He did find it curious, when the same blonde replied "thanks! Will you be joining us?"

"Uh, no, I don't think so" he replied back. And not knowing what else to say, he added "y'all have fun." The two ladies giggled and assured him they were planning on doing just that.

Mystified but not so much as to follow-up on the trio, the Officer continued to clean the unit.

Ten minutes later, another car pulls into the lot. This one is clearly an unmarked unit and it heads straight to the Officer cleaning the Rescue unit. Driving the unit is a Uniformed Captain, whom the Officer readily recognized.

Greetings were exchanged and the Captain asks the Officer where the Sergeant is (the Sergeants unit was sitting right there). The Officer said "I think he went into the gym Captain, however, I'm not certain."

The seasoned Captain had a fairly clear "knowing look" on his face, when he exited his unit and walked to the very door, the Sergeant had disappeared behind, as did both ladies later. At this point, the Officer was finishing up his task of washing the unit, however, curiosity prevented him from leaving the immediate area.

Less than two minutes pass and the aforementioned Captain emerges, alone, carrying what appeared to be a full uniform, including the shoes. He enters his unit, waves at the Officer and drives off.

His curiosity now hitting on all cylinders, there was little chance of anyone prying the Officer from his choice point of observation.

A scant few minutes go by and the Sergeant then appears. However, instead of being attired in the uniform in which he had arrived in, he was now wearing what appeared to be some old uniform pants, that were obviously too small for him, as they couldn't be buttoned at the waist.

He was also barefoot and was hurriedly trying to squeeze into a "Tuffy Jacket," a uniform jacket that is insulated and outfitted with a "fake fur" collar, for cold weather. The Officer found this truly curious, as this time-frame was in mid-summer, in South Louisiana. Nobody, at least nobody in their right mind, wore a Tuffy Jacket this time of the year.

The Sergeant then quickly entered his unit and sped off, following the same path, the Officer noted, as the Captain. Just as he was pondering what may have happened, the two ladies exit the door and head for their car. The Officer seizes the opportunity for some answers.

Walking up to their car, at the same time they arrived at it, the Officer asks "hey ladies, do you know what happened with the Sergeant?" They shrugged and this time, the brunette driver responds with "we're really not sure. He answered his little radio and said something to someone on it. He then said he had to go and quickly got out of the Jacuzzi."

The officer, positive he was looking incredulous, asked "Jacuzzi?"

The blonde giggled and said "oh yeah, we were just having a little fun."

With that, they got into the car and drove off. The ideas swimming through the Officer's head at this point are not suitable for the rating this book will fall under. He makes a mental note to try and find out just what in the world actually took place.

Two, maybe three days go by and the Officer hasn't quite forgotten about the chain of events which he, alone, bore witness to. Then, as luck would have it, he runs into the Sergeant. He says "hey Sarge, if you tell me to mind my own business, I will, however, I'll admit to being a bit more than just a tad curious, as to what transpired."

The Sergeant truly was a happy-go-lucky sort who can seemingly allow any trouble to flow over him, like water off a ducks back. He replied "I don't mind your asking as I bet you are curious. So, I'll tell you."

It seems that his Captain had been "after him" for some time. It wasn't that he was a *screw-up* as much as he was simply talented at doing whatever he wanted to do, at the City's and citizens expense. Being a field Sergeant was akin to giving this over six foot kid, a golden pass-key to the candy store. And since he knew the Captain had him in his cross-hairs, he was all the more careful, making it nigh impossible to catch him doing anything, not to mention doing anything wrong.

In most cases, such as what was just described, *luck* can and will almost certainly run out. This case would prove to be no different.

You see, the Captain called in and told his Lieutenant that he was sick and would not be coming in. This wasn't an unusual occurrence, as it was common for Captain's, what with , ittheir tenure, would routinely burn some sick time, prior to their retiring from the department.

However, unknown to the Lieutenant and most certainly the Sergeant, he did in fact "come in." He just hung out on the perimeter and watched his target, the Sergeant, like a hawk. So, when the Captain "located" him at the school, he waited what proved to be an optimum amount of time and moved in for the "kill."

Truth be known, the Captain thought the escapade would end, right there, on the grounds of the Hollywood complex. However, when he entered the weight room, it seems that he discovered the Sergeant's full uniform lying there, on a weight bench. He altered his plan, on the fly and the Officer had seen him leave with said uniform.

What the Officer, who was playing spectator that day, had no way of knowing, was that the Captain drove a few miles away, to Memorial Stadium, where he then called, on the radio, for the Sergeant to meet him. That was when the Officer saw the Sergeant leave, partially dressed in clothes that he scrounged around and found in the gym.

Upon arriving at Memorial Stadium, he pulls up, side-by-side, with the Captain. Now, remember, the Sergeant is wearing the Tuffy Jacket, complete with *fur* collar.

The Captain greets him, then does a double-take and asks the Sergeant "what in the hell are you wearing?!?" The Sergeant, sweating as profusely as he was involuntarily, replied, "well, I developed a chill, so I put this jacket on."

"A chill; in 90-degree weather, you're telling me you're having *chills*?" demanded the Captain.

Without any warning whatsoever, the Captain places his unit in drive and moves forward, just enough to exit his unit, which he does.

The Captain then directs the Sergeant to exit his unit. The Sergeant said he didn't feel like that was a good idea. The Captain then informed him it wasn't an idea or a suggestion; "get out of your unit."

The Sergeant opens his car door, gingerly steps out, barefooted though he may be, and reaches to hold whomever's trousers up, that he was wearing. Since the jacket was too small to close, it was quite clear that the Sergeant wasn't wearing a shirt.

The Captain looked him over, then walked back to his unit and pulled the Sergeants uniform and shoes from his front seat. He handed them to the Sergeant and instructed him "get dressed, then meet me in my office."

At the time the Sergeant was relaying what took place, to the Officer, he was still in "wait and see" mode as to what the final punishment was going to be. Being the character that he was, he parted with one bit of advice to the Officer.

"Always carry a backup uniform," he said as he grinned, winked and walked off.

14 | Just Shoot It

While it may not be relevant to the story, you may find it interesting to know that two different Officers were interviewed for this piece, and the same story, pretty close to verbatim, emerged.

This took place, sometime around the mid-1980's and one Officer recalls it taking place off of Stevendale Road.

One of BRPD's burglary detectives has a suspect in custody, relative to several burglaries and the suspect is cooperating. That is, he's now at the stage, that he is sitting handcuffed in the rear seat of the Detective's unit and he leading the Detective to where he stashed the goods, for later retrieval.

As the story goes, the Detective and suspect arrive at a wooded location, on Stevendale Road, where, according to the suspect, the goods are stashed some distance off the roadway.

The Detective, being in a "standard sedan" for a unit, recognizes the fact that he won't be able to drive very far into the area, without getting stuck. In looking for a way to recover the goods, without having to physically march into the woods and carry the items out, piecemeal, he calls for the on-duty Rescue unit.

The Rescue units, at the time, were four-wheel drive Ford Broncos, complete with big tires and a good sized winch mounted on front. All-in-all, it was a good call on the part of the Detective who requested it.

Rescue arrives, learns what the mission is and begins "clearing a path." Within a relatively short amount of time, both units are well into the woods, to the point of being out-of-sight from Stevendale traffic.

With a short distance to go, before they reach their objective, the Rescue unit, leading the way, runs into a problem. The Officer driving that unit gets out to see why he's not able to move forward and discovers that his unit has run on top of a "green sapling," a young tree that is still strong and won't break easily.

Instead of breaking, when run over, the tree simply bent over and as the Rescue unit proceeded, the tree tried to "stand back up" about midway under the unit. And it was strong enough to lift the unit in such a way, that traction was no longer in favor of those inside. In other words, the unit stopped. It was going anywhere, as long as that sapling had anything to do with it.

The Officer driving the Rescue unit diagnoses the problem, then walks back and informs the Detective of the situation, thereby seeking any suggestions on what they can do.

The Detective hasn't really been paying any attention to what was taking place in front of him. He was busy writing, recording information that the talkative suspect was willing to share. He looks up, from his position behind the steering wheel of his unit, listens to the "problem" as it's being laid out and replies "just shoot it."

The Rescue Officer looks quizzically at the Detective and says "what?"

The Detective repeats his assertion, saying "just shoot it."

One can assume, for the moment that the Detective had a momentary memory lapse, as to whom he was speaking to. That is, the Rescue Officer.

It was generally known, department-wide, that this individual was as good a person as they came. And he was considered, by many, to be truly gifted in his use of the Jaws-of-Life, especially the many souls he was credited with having extricated from mangled cars.

He was also fairly well known for taking directions quite

literally. So much so, that his superior in Rescue once remarked "I always issue two sets of directions. One for the crew, in general, the other being for *him*."

The Detective would later report that a scant two minutes later, he, along with the suspect (who confessed that he thought he was being taken into the woods to be shot), heard a series of several loud gunshots, in close proximity to where they were sitting.

After jumping out of his unit to investigate, the Detective learned that the Rescue Officers, in taking the Detective's advice, had bent down, looked under the Rescue unit, took aim and opened fire on the sapling.

While it was a little late, for the Detective to inform the Rescue Officer that he wasn't serious when he had said "just shoot it," all present conceded that the solution, while not optimum, was indeed successful. The tree surrendered and the two units were now able to press on to the stashed goods.

This is where the story ends, well, sort of.

Shots fired, throughout the history of the Baton Rouge Police Department, have always been taken seriously, regardless if the shots hit anyone or not. This case proved to be no different, as the Rescue Officer was ultimately given some time off to "think about how he could have better handled the situation."

15 | Fatman and the Root

Now, we find our story situated on what could have been a simple traffic stop. Come to think of it though, if it were *simple*, it wouldn't be a story and it most certainly wouldn't be included in this collection.

Therefore, we'll just settle with it *started* with a traffic stop.

The time frame was late 1980's, perhaps early 1990's. One of the two Officer's involved, who shared this story, wasn't certain. And the time in history is of really no significance anyway.

One male Officer, one female Officer and the two end up stopping a guy on N. Lobdell, in Baton Rouge, in the parking lot of the Copper Ridge Apartments. One of the Officers has the violator leaning against the front-end of his car, as the secondary Officer is conducting a warrants check, via portable radio.

Everything is fine, right up until the portable radio comes alive, with the information that the violator has an outstanding active misdemeanor *traffic* warrant. Instantly, the guy bolts and runs. The male Officer that was with him grabs the guy and they "dance" a little bit, to the point that the Officer pulls the suspects shirt off.

Now, it's important, right here, to understand that when *anyone* runs from the police, the police are going to run after them! It's just the way it is. Yes, it was a misdemeanor traffic warrant, however, at this point, he may as well have been Charles Manson and the Officers having been informed that Manson had just escaped. He's going down!

The male Officer takes off after the suspect and the chase is on. The female officer is running behind and with the male Officer, in pursuit. In less than a minute, the male Officer reported hearing the female Officer, now on the radio with HQ, that her partner is in foot pursuit.

To her credit, she gives a really good description of the suspect. Perhaps it should read "*a really too good of a description*" as she informs HQ "and the suspect is really FAT HQ, I mean, REALLY FAT." And she continues with her play-by-play call of the pursuit, with the direction and occasional "he's really very fat HQ, approaching units can't miss him."

At some point about this time, her male partner, who realizes that the suspect evidently feels more vested in getting away, than he does in catching him, turns and yells at his partner to "cut the fat crap; I can't catch the fat bastard!!"

The Officer sees the suspect head in between two apartment buildings and catches up to him. Just as the Officer reaches out to push the guy to the ground, tackle him or whatever, to end the chase, his foot runs across the unseen root of a Live Oak tree. Within a layer of fabric of catching the guy, the pursuing Officer finds himself doing a rather ugly flip. As he is "chicken flipping" end-over-end to ultimately land on his backside, he hears his partner, still with the play-by-play, tell HQ "my partner just went down on a root!"

In the end, the suspect was eventually cornered in an empty apartment and arrested. Fortunately, the only injury suffered during the episode was to the male Officer's pride.

16 | In Pursuit...ahhhh

In the early 1980's, if you rode out of the old Broadmoor Precinct on Sharp Road, you had but one choice as to where you could re-fuel (as did every other police unit in Baton Rouge at the same time). That was "City Lot" located on Chippewa Street, across from G. N. Gonzalez (motorcycles).

More often than not, units from Broadmoor would jump on the interstate and head out to get fueled up. Typically speaking, most everyone would wait towards the end of the shift, after eight hours of patrolling and answering calls, to go get fuel. Generally speaking, this would serve two purposes.

First, it would "tie" you up, with HQ, as they wouldn't give you a call until you refueled and secondly, you would pass your unit to the relieving shift, with a near-full tank. Such was the case, when two Officers, riding together, got up on I-12 and steered towards City Lot.

The Officers were near the end of their shift and were trying to judge if they had enough fuel to even make it to City Lot. It appeared to the driver that the "E" on their gas gauge and the gas gauge needle were sure getting friendly.

Just as they had convinced each other they could make the journey with an ounce or two to spare, both Officers spotted a white-colored station wagon traveling at an extremely high rate of speed.

They spotted the wagon headed west on I-10 (coming out of the direction of New Orleans), as they were headed west on I-12, approaching the same intersection (10/12 split) as the wagon. At one point they parallel to one another and they thought perhaps that the driver would see their unit and slow down. So much for thinking.

As opposed to slowing, it appeared the wagon's driver gunned it as the vehicle began leaving the Officers in their Chevrolet Malibu. Now, as mentioned in a previous story, it's difficult, if not impossible to ignore something so blatant. And such was the case for our "dynamic duo."

The red lights came on and the chase was on. "HQ, we're headed west on I-10 approaching the LSU lakes, in pursuit of a solid white station wagon."

HQ put it out and when it became clear that the wagon was committed to heading west over the new bridge, HQ informed the Officers that the West Baton Rouge Parish Sheriff's Office was waiting at the bottom of the bridge. Both Officers had been around long enough to know how *warm* of a welcome WBRSO afforded potential suspects headed to their turf, so they wisely backed off a notch on the gas pedal, hoping to save one or two wisps of fumes for use to get their much-needed fuel.

Just prior to reaching the bridge's summit, HQ announced that WBRSO had the *suspect* stopped and said suspect proved to be a Louisiana State Trooper enroute to a rape scene, in another Parish.

Now, the two Officers who had initiated the "chase," heard the radio transmission about it being a Trooper, *prior* to reaching the location where the stop was made. They kept driving, looking as curious as everyone else that was on the scene and doubled-back, continuing their original journey for fuel.

To this day, as far as they know, nobody but them and the dispatcher knows for certain who started that little fiasco.

17 | Grosse Tete Handoff

This story has its beginnings in the 2nd District area of Baton Rouge (the LSU area for brevity) in about 1992.

The Officer in this story was regularly assigned to zone 2-A, which, for the sake of this piece, covers downtown Baton Rouge, south of Florida Street, well south of LSU and also encompasses the new bridge.

It's evening shift and it's been a busy evening shift. And for the third or fourth time, this particular Officer is dispatched to a guy on Government Street that is harassing the citizens that are tied up in traffic.

It appeared he was working his way up and down Government Street as the day before he had been in the vicinity of the McDonalds, where he was enjoying terrorizing the eatery's customers.

This time, though, he was under the I-110 overpass, on the eastbound lane of Government. The Officer arrives and is frustrated to see it's the same individual, who, at the time, knew he couldn't be taken to jail, as there was no space for misdemeanor arrests. And just in case the Officer might have forgotten that fact, the clown happily reminded him. A summons was useless, as he ignored them anyway. So, it appeared to be somewhat of a "stalemate."

About a minute after arriving on the scene, the Officer see his field supervisor, a Sergeant, driving up. The Sergeant exits his unit and asks "him again?"

"Yep, and he knows there's not a whole lot that can done," replied the Officer in return. "Unless, I'm granted a little leeway, we'll get called back out here, again, on this same turkey."

The Sergeant took a drag off his cigarette, exhaled and said "do what you gotta do, I'll put you 10-6 (busy); just contact me when you're done."

With that, the Officer loaded his "passenger" into the back seat of his unit, while being verbally reminded that he could not arrest him.

The Officer just looked at the guy in his rearview mirror, smiled and said "oh, I'm not taking you to jail, we're just going for a ride." And less than a minute later, they were westbound, headed across the new bridge.

It didn't take long for the Officer to begin to wonder just what he could do with his "fare," after leaving the bridge into Port Allen, still westbound on I-10.

A couple of miles went by, when it occurred to the Officer that the little community of Grosse Tete was roughly twenty miles ahead. He continued west on the interstate until he saw the junction of Highway 77 ahead. Now, Highway 77, at one time, was a well-used north-south roadway. It was still in use, albeit mainly by locals, as it was considered to be a dangerous 2-lane highway with virtually no shoulders to speak of.

At the intersection, the Officer turned north, noting that his passenger had not uttered a peep since leaving Baton Rouge behind.

Highway 77 was not only a lonely stretch of highway, at this time of night, it was also quite dark. Aside from the headlights on the unit, there was no ambient light to be seen anywhere.

The Officer stopped his unit in the northbound lane and exited. He opened the rear passenger door of his unit and directed his rider to "get out." The guy refused. He told the Officer "you're gonna shoot me and leave me here."

Well, the Officer thought "now, there's an idea" but didn't

say it. Instead, he said "get out NOW." The guy slowly emerged, got both feet on the ground and backed away from the Officer. The Officer closes the rear door, gets back into his unit and heads back to the city, where he contacts his Sergeant.

When they met up, the Sergeant said "I just want to know two things. Is he still alive and are we going to be bothered by him again this evening?"

"He's very much alive and not even hurt in any way. And no, I feel it's safe to say that he won't bother us again this evening and there's about a 90% chance tomorrow will be clear as well."

The Sergeant looked somewhat quizzically at the Officer, took a drag off his cigarette and said "okay, you have my curiosity up, what did you do with him?"

"I let him out on Highway 77, about five miles north of Grosse Tete" replied the Officer.

The Sergeant busted out laughing and said "hell, we not hear from him for the rest of the week! Good deal and good riddance."

It would be a pretty good ending right here, huh? I mean, this story has a little bit of everything in it, even the "good guys" winning in the end right? Well, I suppose it would be, however, this isn't quite the end of this story. No, this story carries over until the next day. The setting: roll call at 2nd District on Highland Road.

Roll call ends and the Sergeant pulls the Officer to the side and asks "have you read today's paper?"

"No, I haven't. Is there something in there that would interest me?" asked the Officer.

With that, the Sergeant produces a copy of the *Morning Advocate* and points to a specific story, whose setting was in Shreveport, Louisiana.

The story was somewhat detailed, however, the gist of it was this. Two police officers in Shreveport were under investigation on a potential charge of kidnapping. It seems that they were experiencing a similar issue, only with a drunk.

They allegedly loaded the drunk up and took him to a neighboring town, where they dropped him off. One major difference is that the lone police Officer, in that town, happened to also be the town's Police Chief. When he ran across the drunk and deciphered how it was that he (the drunk) got there, the Chief returned the favor.

Therein begins the he said, they said exchange and the whole scenario ended up on the desk of the District Attorney. Even though, the DA, at that time, was somehow related to the aforementioned Police Chief, there was no finger pointing.

The Sergeant looked at me and said, "well, it's a little different, however, for the sake of any potential problems, I think that should be the last trip out-of-town."

The Officer readily agreed and left for his tour of duty.

Now, as a footnote, for those that are interested in this sort of thing; the guy that went with the Officer to Grosse Tete was indeed spotted several days later, back in Baton Rouge, near Government and St. Louis. He was never a problem again.

18 | Woodn't You Know It?

We're going to head back out to Broadmoor for this one. This is about 1981. Baton Rouge has a new Mayor and a new Chief of Police. And, as always been the case, new changes within the department.

Just as a reminder, that by and large, the Officers are driving the little Chevrolet Malibus, with the small but energetic 350 4-barrel under the hood.

Roll call is over and two male Officers, riding together, head out for their assigned unit. On the way out of the Precinct, the drive tells his partner, "we've got to make a couple of stops first, before we get into anything." Of course the partner says "sure" and as he walks to the unit, he (the partner) notices that the unit appears as though the back-end is all but out, as the front bumper is pointing towards the sky.

He dutifully points this fact out to the driver who looks and says "naw, its fine. Let's go."

They head out and eventually pull into the parking lot of *Sonny's Bar-B-Que* on Florida Blvd. They head straight to the back, where, at the time, was a relatively small fenced-in area, containing firewood. The Officer that is driving pulls in front of a gate to this area, and backs up to the gate. He then gets out and walks to the trunk of the police unit and opens the trunk.

All the while his partner is sitting on the passenger side of the unit, filling out the top part of their "trip sheet." The partner, still in the unit, hears a sharp rap on the unit; then hears his partner ask "are you going to come back here and help me?" The Officer exits the unit and walks back to the rear of it, looks in the trunk and sees that it's full of firewood.

He looks at his partner and asks "what are you doing?"

"I'm bringing them their delivery of firewood, what does it look like I'm doing? Now, grab some and pass it to me as this job will go a lot faster with two of us."

And so, they emptied half of the firewood there, at which time the Officer riding "shotgun" was told "that's enough." They then hit the road again and headed to the *Hickory Stick*, another bar-b-que restaurant, this one on Airline Highway. At that location, the remaining firewood was off-loaded and the duo wet 10-8 (in-service).

The Officer relating this story (shotgun Officer) says that he still thinks about that delivery every time he and his family eat at Sonny's.

19 | The Devil Made Me Do It

The year was 1996. The setting; the Homicide/Robbery Office located at the then BPRD HQ at 704 Mayflower Street. At the time, Ted Kaczynski aka *The Unabomber*, was in the news, as he had recently been apprehended after a twenty-year domestic terrorism run (he mailed bombs to various people).

It's common knowledge throughout the department, that when the folks in Homicide get called out, they truly earn their pay. Long days and long hours was and still are the norm for that particular assignment. On the other hand, during the rare "down-times," and especially after all reports are caught up with, Detectives can be a little pressed in curbing their pent-up energy. And the latter is more-or-less, what led up to *The Devil Made Me Do It*.

It's important for the reader to know that the Bureau Commander, over Homicide/Robbery and several other Divisions as well, was also an active member of SRT (Special Response Team), maintaining a leadership role in that group as well.

One other little detail, which some who read this will immediately recognize, therefore, this is for those who aren't as familiar with the particular packages.

Throughout the Criminal Investigation Bureau (CIB), where one would expect to find a Division such as Homicide/Robbery, supervisors would order the Detectives the special notepads that were as tall as a steno pad, yet narrow so as to fit in a coat pocket and/or be easily held in one's hand. These notepads would come twenty to a pack and a pack was simply twenty such pads, wrapped neatly in brown packing paper.

Now, one of the little brown packages, of notepads, measuring roughly 8 inches – 9 inches in length, maybe 5 inches high and 4 inches wide, in and of itself, was a non-threatening inanimate object. It would take a mischievous soul or in this particular case, two such souls, to make that little package any more than what it was; a harmless collection of notepads.

Don't get ahead of me; allow me to put the *formula* together for you.

Two enterprising, somewhat free-spirited Detectives enter the office on what is thus far, a slow day shift. They're both caught up on their work and may have been discussing the apprehension of the much talked about Harvard educated Unabomber.

Regardless of what they were doing when they walked in and spied the previously described notepad package, sitting harmlessly on the secretary's desk; that much of the story is moot anyway. It's what happened afterwards that made for a less-than-boring day.

It really doesn't matter who initially had the idea to stick red and black colored wires into and out of the brown packed notepads. Nor does it matter who wrote the address and name of the CIB Bureau Commander on said package, where one would place such a name, if one were mailing a package to someone.

If fact, it doesn't matter who, in the "From" section (upper left-hand corner) of the same package, wrote "*Unabomber*" and placed the described parcel on the aforementioned Commander's desk. No sir and no ma'am, none of that matters.

What does matter is what took place no later than ten minutes after the "gift" was discovered on that desk, by the very person who was assigned to that office. That's right. The Bureau Commander walked in and the first thing he sees, prior to a cup of coffee being brought to his lips, was what all of his training and all of the videos he had ever seen said it was, a *bomb*.

Now, as one might expect from a highly trained, very detailed and thorough Commander, there was absolutely no hesitation on his part. He acted calmly (the jury remains out on this one detail to this day) and quickly. He immediately notified the various members of SRT, who themselves were in various stages of getting ready to report to work or just getting ready for bed, after a long night of work. In the department, it's known as *call-out*. Once you get called out, you go to where you're needed; in this case, the CIB Commander's Office at HQ.

At this point you may be wondering about our two *bored* Detectives, whose inspiration makes this story what it is. Well, they are just a few yards away, in the Homicide/Robbery Office, preparing a pot of coffee, getting settled into whatever the day may bring, when *delivery* comes via the police radio.

Our two pranksters hear SRT being dispatched to HQ, for what appears to be a bomb in the CIB Commanders Office. They look at each other and the color drains from of their faces. The other one breaks out in a raucous fit of laughter, seeking to high-five his fellow culprit, who is fast appearing green around the gills.

The entire situation is flowing off the laughing one like water off a ducks back. The less-than-confident Detective informs his partner that he must go and confess, so that the *Calvary* can be withdrawn.

"NO! Don't say a word, much less tell him we did it!!" exclaimed the one still fighting with bouts of laughter.

"But I must, otherwise, he's really going to be pissed" replied the one who kept seeing his career flash before his eyes.

"Nobody will ever figure out what they're not told!!" Mr. *Cool* asserted.

In the end, the nervous half of the team succumbed and confessed, although he admirably shouldered the blame, leaving his accomplice completely out of it. His partner, shaking his head in disbelief, struggled with "*I told you so*" when the Commander ordered a full investigation, with threats of *heads will roll* floating through the hallways.

It was later suggested that the nervous Detective, who was known for his liberal use of *Jergen's Lotion* (to keep his hands smooth), got the bottle of lotion confused with a bottle of *Maalox*, the latter being used just as liberally as the lotion, to settle his stomach during the course of the aforementioned investigation. That rumor was never confirmed.

Ultimately, the investigation was withdrawn almost as abruptly as it had been started. No disciplinary measures were ever doled out, as the idea was that the *lone suspect* in the matter had endured enough.

While there was little doubt that he had indeed suffered enough, he still faced the daily onslaught of ribbing from his partner, for quite some time.

20 | The Governmental Building

In 1992, one of the duties that still fell to Officers working out of 2nd District (Highland Road), was "building security." To many, it was a loathsome detail, in that one basically sat behind the security desk at the Governmental Building, located at 222 St. Louis St. and "watched it." On the evening shift and weekends, many would have preferred watching grass grow or paint peel before entering "the tomb."

On one particular evening shift, however, things were looking to be made a little "livelier," especially for the new rookie who was going to get his first taste of building security. In fact, the process of putting the rookie in the "right frame of mind" began several hours before he was to relieve another Officer (who was in on the plan) at the building.

The rookies FTO (Field Training Officer), who, as far as the rookie knew and was concerned, was straitlaced, informed his rookie about the assignment shortly after leaving roll call for patrol.

Naturally, the rookie had some questions, as what his duties would be at the building and what he should expect. His FTO was happy to oblige in answering his questions.

"It's really a somewhat boring job" the FTO explained. "If there are any late trials going on upstairs (the building included several City Parish Offices as well as the 19th JDC), you may have to let the occasion juror or witness out through the front door, as you will be the only one with a key. Aside from that, well, that and the sounds, it's really going to be a challenge to not die of boredom."

The rookie, hanging on to *every* word, nods, then asks "sounds? What sounds do you mean?"

"Did I say that? Sounds, I mean? Sorry, I was thinking about the last few times I had to cover the building. No biggie."

The rookie doesn't respond at first, then finally his curiosity got the best of him. "What kind of sounds are you referring to? Did you hear something I mean, that I need to know about?"

"Well" the FTO exhales and *reluctantly* agrees to explain to his young trainee, "it's fairly common knowledge that the Governmental Building was built upon a Civil War cemetery. I mean, it wasn't known at the time of construction but when the contractors began unearthing human remains, and forensics experts identified the remains as soldiers from the Civil War, *then* it became known."

At this point the FTO has the rookies 100% undivided attention. "You mean, the building actually sits on top of an old cemetery?"

"Awwww, heck, it's better than that! The desk where you'll be sitting is directly over what appeared to experts to have been a mass grave. How's **that** for some history, huh?"

The rookie, in an almost inaudible whisper replies "yeah, boy." Then, in a little stronger voice, asks "well, what kinda sounds were you referring to earlier?

The FTO, using his most helpful, *fatherly* voice he can muster at the time, says "well, the building is big you know and well, sometimes one thinks he hears something; you know, that's not really there. Heck, you may even go through the entire evening without hearing anything."

"What do you mean by *hear something that's not there?*" implores the Rookie.

"Well, like I said, it's a big building. Sometimes you might hear something and when you go to locate the cause of the sound, there's nothing there. That's happened to me before but, as I also said, you may go through the entire evening without hearing a thing."

Now, I must interject here, that telling the Rookie that he may not hear anything during his tour at the building, was about as absurd as suggesting it in the first place. The truth of the matter was just what and how much he was going to hear. He was definitely not destined to make it through the evening unscathed.

The appointed hour had arrived and the FTO pointed his unit in the direction of 222 St. Louis Street. His reluctant hero partner, the Rookie, had *reluctant* locked up tighter than a drum.

Upon arriving at the building, the FTO escorted the Rookie inside and let the Officer there know he was being relieved. The Rookie seized the opportunity to ask that Officer "did you hear anything?"

This Officer, who was in on the prank, replied "nothing more than usual," and began walking in the direction of the exit.

The Rookie looked at his FTO and said "oh wonderful."

The FTO looked at him and said "you'll be fine. Just remember, I'll pick you up here, at the end of the shift. Besides, if you need something, I'm a radio call away." And with that, the FTO left the Rookie, alone and "in charge" of security for an imposing mausoleum-like structure.

Now, it's important for the reader to know that where the Rookie (and everyone who is assigned to security for the building) would be stationed, is on the first/ground floor of the building. The front doors to the complex are some 40-feet or so from the security desk and on the easternmost wall.

The security desk itself is situated just inside the "rear doors," on the westernmost wall, facing the Mississippi River. Directly in front of the security desk is a staircase, leading down to the B-1 (Basement 1) and B-2 (Basement 2) levels. It's also important for you, the reader, to know that one can drive a car (unit) into a parking garage, which is on the B-1 level, below ground and directly below the westernmost wall and security desk.

One can exit their vehicle in this garage, walk into the building at the B-1 level without ever having to go upstairs to be seen by anyone. That is, anyone with a key, which the FTO and the other Officer just happened to have.

The Rookie was given just enough "down-time" to begin getting comfortable with his new surroundings. He would report later that the first thing he heard was the sound of "troops" marching, somewhere in the bowels of the building. Never let it be said that the Rookie didn't have an active imagination. His FTO never could figure out how the sound of two people walking on granite floors could be discerned as "troops."

It wasn't until the Officer that he had relieved, had actually gone to the bottom of the stairs; the same stairs that were situated in front of the security desk, and made some rather unique sounds that prompted the Rookie to yell down the staircase "challenging" whatever it was he was hearing.

They would give him a break, providing a "lull" in the "hauntings" and then they would begin with another round of unexplained phenomena. Through it all, the Rookie maintained his station.

And then it happened.

The westernmost wall of the Governmental Building, on the ground floor, is predominately glass. It steel framework, supporting the glass in stages or frames, it's almost one long window pane, facing the river. As mentioned previously, the security desk sits just below and a few feet from this window.

At one point, with the Rookies attention fully pointed in another direction, the Officer whom he had relieved had made his way to the ground floor, just outside of this window.

Peeking in and seeing that the Rookie was looking in another direction, he slapped the window with his open palm. The openness and high ceiling of the ground floor offers a reverberating echo effect, which can be underscored with absolutely no foot traffic in the building.

This proved to be the "icing on the cake." The Rookie contacts his FTO via radio and asks to see him. The FTO drives from the aforementioned B-1 garage and makes the block, coming up to the front of the building where he sees his Rookie sitting curbside, holding a portable police radio and a PR-24 (police nightstick).

The FTO pulls up and maintaining straight face, asks "what's going on?"

The Rookie emphatically states that was his first and last time to work building security, regardless of the ramifications. He figured if the Civil War ghosts wanted the property back that badly, who was he to argue with them.

It took a little convincing but after they described the very sounds he had heard, the Officers officially announced that the Rookie was suitably initiated among their ranks.

That Rookie is now a Lieutenant, fast headed to retirement. And yes, he still remembers that evening.

21 | Transferred

In 1981, at the old Broadmoor Precinct on Sharp Road, there was a squad of Officers who worked well together. That's not to say there were not several more such squads, throughout the department, at the time; however, for the setting of this story, the focus is on one squad in particular.

January 1981 brought some changes to the department. Baton Rouge had a new Mayor and with a new Mayor, comes a new Chief of Police. A new Chief typically has some different ideas on how to run the department, therefore the changes trickle down to the various Divisions and Precincts and ultimately, the Officers themselves.

At this time as well, rumors about changes, as well as the actual changes, were pretty much a dime-a-dozen. In other words, they were everywhere. Now, for those reading this, that have never worked in such a climate as a police precinct, one such change that is periodically discussed are transfers.

That is, transferring one or more Officers to another squad, at the same precinct or worse yet, to a whole different squad/shift at a different precinct. And for any number of reasons, such moves took place, not often but they did take place.

Such was the atmosphere, for the setting of this story. Rumors of transfers were running more rampant than ever before. The very thought of being moved from a squad that worked so well together, where coming to work was actually fun, well, that seemed downright criminal.

It didn't help that two Officers who worked closely together on this squad, we "fanning the flames" of the rumor mill. More precisely, they were fanning the flames in the direction of one Rookie in particular. This Rookie had already heard the rumors concerning transfers and made the mistake of telling our two "heroes" of his concerns. Well, there's nothing like a good friend, or as in this case, "friends" helping out in your "Maalox moment."

These two Officers put their heads together and felt that a "transfer" was in order. They knew the transfer had to look, feel and "smell" official, otherwise, the efforts of putting together a classic prank would be for naught. And they certainly couldn't have that!

One of the two Officers made his way to 300 North Blvd., which at the time was Baton Rouge Police HQ. While downtown for court, he wandered into the Chief's Office and contacted on of the Chief's secretaries.

He, in fact, told her what his mission was. To provide a "letter of transfer" to a specific Officer, complete on the Chief's letterhead and in the white #10 envelope that was marked "Chief's Office." He asked for the envelope and letterhead, saying that he would actually type the letter himself.

This particular secretary smiled broadly and said "you're bad. However, let me ask you this. You do plan on telling him it's a joke, don't you?"

"Oh but of course! We wouldn't actually let him report to work at the new location." (only because they had not thought it through that far)

The secretary smiled and said, well, it's got to look official, so I'll type you one out real quick," and she did. Oh, it was a beauty. The Officer couldn't wait to show his buddy what truly was an official transfer, with the one exception being the Chief had no idea of its existence.

Armed with the letter, he reported for work that afternoon and showed his accomplice the "jewel" in letter form. They both marveled that not only was the latter in an official envelope from the Chief's Office, the letter also bore the Chief's stamped "signature" which effectively erased any hint of it being a complete forgery.

They then placed the envelope into the target's mailbox, in the roll call room. The only thing left to do now, was wait. Fortunately, they didn't wait long, as five minutes later, their target walked in and as most do Officer are inclined to do, walked straight to his mailbox and retrieved the envelope.

Both Officers were watching him, like hawks, yet trying to appear as they were doing anything but. They watched as he looked at the envelope and saw his head drop to his chest, without his having even opened it to see what the envelope contained. He appeared as he didn't have on ounce of air left in him as he walked to the back of the room, waiting for roll call to commence.

Once at the back of the room, he opened the envelope, slid the letter out and read it. It was then that both Officers "noticed" that something was awry and asked him, "are you okay?"

Without saying a single word, he handed the letter to one of the Officers who read it, despite knowing every word of it already. The transfer was from Broadmoor Precinct to Winbourne Precinct, in North Baton Rouge. For the uninitiated, the letter essentially said "we're moving you from a slow area to the single busiest area for police, in all of Baton Rouge."

Well, all his two buds could offer at a time like this were general condolences and "it's been nice knowing you."

The man couldn't tell you what took place in roll call that day. His eyes watered and as soon as roll call ended, he exited without a word.

Now folks, understand this. The shift Commander, a Captain, was in on the joke, therefore, he had been watching the target's reaction as well. When he saw him exit the building, he approached the two others and said "Y'all best go and tell him it's a joke. I'd hate to see him get hurt because he thinks he's being moved."

While that wasn't the original plan (the original plan was to let him stew for a few hours), the two Officers noted the wisdom in what the Captain said and they walked out behind their buddy.

Outside, they called him by name, prompting him to pause. They caught up with him and confirmed that telling him the truth was the thing to do. He was ready to resign. His day, at this point was totally ruined. In fact, he was seriously considering the idea of leaving for the day.

The Officers looked at each other and chuckled, then told him the truth. The only thing was he wasn't buying it. He said something to the effect, "oh, nice try guys but this is it. I'm done. I don't bother anyone and now this."

It took the two Officers having to lay out, in detail, as to how the letter came to exist. Well, he looked at them with a glimmer of hope; that is hope they were being honest with him for once in their lives. He cocked his head and asked them "who else knows about this?"

At that point the back door to the Precinct opened and out popped the Captain. The Officer's nodded to him said, "just the Captain."

The targeted Officer looked over at the Captain, who was grinning while pulling a cigar from his shirt pocket. The Captain said "I told them they needed to tell you the truth."

For a brief few minutes, he was mad. The two Officers were "slime buckets" and a few other things that don't print well. However, when the two Officers pointed out to him "Ain't it nice knowing you're really going to stay here with us?"

He tried to looked peeved but instead, he grinned and said "yeah, I guess so. I'll admit that's one of the better ones I've seen you two come up with. I would have enjoyed it better though, had it been played on someone else and I was a spectator!"

Those were some fun times.

22 | Messin' With the Truckers

This next *event*, without a doubt, should have been recorded. It will be long-remembered as one of the single funniest gags anyone has ever pulled.

It's about 1993 and the setting is the 2nd District area (Highland Road and beyond). During this time, it was popular, among Officers and most of the first-level supervisors (Sergeants), to conduct most of their non-official communication, on CB (citizen-band) radios. Doing so served several purposes, i.e., freeing up the police radio for important traffic and perhaps, most of all, provided Officers with the freedom of saying things they couldn't afford to say on "official" recorded police frequencies.

There were two Officers, in particular, who "ran the roads" together on a regular basis. They were known as proactive Officers in that, they generally could locate solid dope deals and consistently made quality felony arrests. And sometimes, when things were slow, they also knew how to have fun. Such was the case on this one dog shift.

One of the Officers, a likable, good looking guy who enjoyed life in general, seemed to always have a mischievous air about him. Some believe that air came from the ever-present smile on his face. Others attributed it to the fact that he hailed from New Orleans. Regardless, he was and is a great guy who was most capable of pulling a prank.

Now, this Officer could also disguise his voice in such a manner that he could maintain his range, so that he sounded almost like a woman. This evening he was sitting side-by-side with his "running partner," talking, when they heard what was obviously a trucker, on the nearby "super-slab" (interstate), on "their" (the Officers) CB frequency.

At the time, most truckers and anyone else traveling on the open highways across America and who had access to a CB, would primarily stay on and monitor "channel 19" aka "the truckers channel." On occasion however, just to take a conversation off the "main channel" it wasn't uncommon for truckers and others to "drop down" to a lesser used channel. This very thing took place, while these two Officers were sitting stationary, in a parking lot, chatting.

Neither of the two Officers recall what the truckers were talking about at the time and frankly, that's irrelevant to the side-splitting events that followed.

Our New Orleans native smiled, winked at his partner and said "watch this."

He picked up his CB microphone and sending his voice up to the rafters, as far as octaves go, informed the truckers "now boys, you're going to have to go back to 19 or find another channel to talk about how good your wives are. Us men are on this channel and we like to talk alone."

Well, there was a half-a-breath of silence followed by "why you flippin' fruit! Meet me and I'll show you what a real man looks like!!"

By now both Officers were grinning from ear-to-ear, when the one replied "oh, my, would you? Are you serious?"

The trucker responded "am I serious? 'Bout what?"

"Oh, don't crawfish on me now, you said you would show me what a real man looks like if I agreed to meet you."

The trucker replied "oh, you'd better believe it. You want to see what a real man looks like sweet thang, you meet me at mile-marker 141 (some number anyway) on the 10 side after the split, east bound. I'll be waitin' on ya."

"I'm on my way sugar!! I can't wait!!"

"Neither can I" the trucker responded.

Now, at this point the two Officers put their units in motion and head towards mile-marker 141. They arrive, within minutes and sure enough, there's an eighteen-wheeler, pulled to the shoulder, with its hazard lights flashing. The two units pull up behind the truck and ignite their bar lights.

The trucker exits his cab and meets the two Officers at the rear of his rig. The Officer, who had initiated the CB conversation, although that fact wasn't known by the trucker, asks "is everything okay? Is your truck broken down?"

"Oh no, Officer," the big rig operator replied, "I just pulled over, ya know, gettin' a little tired," and chuckled nervously while looking back down the interstate, beyond where the Officers had parked their units.

"Well, yeah, we certainly understand that but for safety's sake, you can't pull over on the shoulder. You need to stop at a rest stop, weigh station, truck stop, you know, somewhere off the beaten path where it's safer for all concerned" suggested the Officer.

"Yes sir, I do know what you mean. In fact, I'll move it right now. I do appreciate that Officer," and with that the trucker returned to the cab of his rig and kicked it into gear.

The lead Officer smiled and said "now it gets good." Both

Officers piled back into their units and pulled away.

The CB comes to life once again, with the one Officer using his high-pitched voice asking "hey sugar, where'd you go? I'm at mile-marker 141 and I don't see anyone, much less a real man."

The truck instantly replies "two city-kitties saw me and made me leave. Hold on to what'cha got, I'm stopping again."

"Okay Boo, just tell me where and I'll be there. I can't wait to see you flex" the Officer responded with a broad grin. The second Officer was trying to catch his breath from laughing so hard.

"Oh yeah, I've got your flex for you, just come on down to marker 146. You won't be disappointed" the trucker promised his supposed target.

"I'm on my way Daddy." And with that, both Officers headed out to mile-marker 146. Sure enough, just as before, the same truck was there, only this time, the operator was already out and standing behind the rig.

After exiting their units behind the truck, the Officers walked up and looking as surprised as two people, who were anything but surprised, could, they said "you again?"

This time, the trucker, who was looking a little sheepish, informed the Officers that he pulled off from where he had previously been and had driven less than a mile, when a warning light came on. He added something about one of his trailer tires and he was in the process of checking them, when the Officers "spotted" him again.

After confirming that everything seemed to be in working order, the two Officers sent their beleaguered "trucker friend" on his way once again.

Two minutes later, a familiar high-pitched voice is heard on the airwaves. "Well, what kind of man stands his date up TWICE? Here I am again and no man in sight. And don't give me any nonsense about a local-yokel making you leave, as I've not seen any around. I just don't think you have what it takes to handle Ready Reggie."

With that, a string of profanities a "mile long" flew from the trucker. It was clear to anyone listening that he had had enough of "Ready Reggie," the "city kitties" and stopping at mile markers.

Less than two weeks later, a memo came out, which was shared at roll call. The memo warned Officers about using profanity on *any* radio and also stated that various CB frequencies were being monitored.

One had to be genuinely creative to have fun......

23 | Office With a Throne

This story comes to us, from one of law enforcement's recognized "king of the prankster's." It (the story) also hails from 1980 and the East Baton Rouge Parish Sheriff's Office.

Allow me to list the *ingredients* of this recipe, followed by how it is prepared.

First off, the location for this particular caper is the old Sheriff's Office, which is now City Court in downtown Baton Rouge. It's a slow, boring night shift and two bored souls come together, in the form of Deputies.

That's not enough to make a good recipe of anything, however, if you throw in an unnamed Captain, who happens to head the IA (Internal Affairs) Division, the flavoring begins to improve.

Now, combine the above with the fact that said Captain isn't well thought of throughout the office, along with the fact that he's just had a brand-new personalized office sign hung on his front door; all that's left is to put this gumbo on a slow cook and wait.

Our two bored, wayward souls spot the new sign and it becomes immediately obvious to one of them, that the sign, although new, would look much better at a new location.

The second floor of the Sheriff's Office, in 1980, was where Administration was located. That is, the Sheriff himself, the Chief Deputy and an assorted group of others whose jobs had them at home, and therefore, away, from the office on nights, holiday's, etc.

In short, there was nobody around to witness the new personalized IA sign, get pulled from the door on which it was displayed in the basement and ferried to the second floor.

After arriving on the second floor, there was nobody, yet again, to witness the sign being glued to its new *home*, that new home being the middle stall of the men's room on that floor. And so it was, relieving our two bored pranksters of that boredom, for a good thirty minutes.

You may be thinking this probably wasn't a good idea and you'd be right. Allow me to assure you, you would be right.

The Deputy whose idea it was initially, headed out of town the next day on a pre-arranged vacation. It turned out to be a good move, as the head of IA, back home, was looking *everywhere* for him. Word got back to our *fugitive* that his job was in jeopardy.

To most folks, this would be a good time to do some serious worrying. Not this one though. It's truly rare to see him with his feathers ruffled and this didn't come close. Why? Well, while he was out of town, *on the lam*, as it were, his parents called him to let him know that the Baton Rouge Police Department had called. Provided he wanted the job they were offering, it was his.

He resigned from EBRSO before anyone, let alone a furious IA Commander, could fire him. Oh but those "left behind" sure appreciated the laughs they got out of it.

24 | Letting the Air Out

It's 1989 and at the time, the Baton Rouge Police Burglary and Narcotics Divisions had not too long before, moved to their new "homes" on Plank Road in Baton Rouge. Specifically, they had taken up residence in what had become known as the CIB (Criminal Investigation Bureau) Annex, situated behind 1st District.

There were other divisions located in the same building as well. Armed Robbery, Forgery and Pawn Shop also had offices there. However, as far as our story goes, we'll focus on the Burglary and Narcotics Divisions. It's also important to know, that there was a traditional "rivalry" between the two divisions.

This friendly rivalry included competing against each other during requalification at the Pistol Range, football games, golf matches and just about anything else where a team effort could be put to the test.

For you to fully appreciate this story, one more important detail needs to be known. That is, one of the secretaries (there were two) in the Narcotics Division, drove a tan colored car, which just happened to be the same color and make as one of the units, the latter assigned to a Narcotics supervisor.

One morning, a Narcotics Detective arrives at the office and heads for the side door, the entrance used by all employees in the building. Prior to reaching the door, he noticed movement several yards away and just in front of a large bay door, which led to an enclosed storage area, all in the same building.

Moving, unobserved, so as to see what was going on, he watched as one of the Burglary supervisors was letting the air out of all four tires, on a tan colored car. This Detective then went on in and the first person he saw was the aforementioned supervisor, whose unit matched the description of the car, whose air was now being depleted.

The Detective asked his supervisor where he was parked.

The supervisor replied "out in front of the bay, why?"

When the Detective told him why he was asking, one could almost feel the "thought processing" mold itself into something tangible.

A scant couple of minutes later, the inside door leading to the storage area, with the bay door, opened, and in walked the Burglary supervisor who had unknowingly been seen by the Narcotics Detective. He didn't say a word, as he walked to his office, the latter being situated in the very rear of the building.

A plan was hatched between the Narcotics Detective and supervisor. They waited but five minutes to put it in motion.

When all was ready, the Narcotics Detective walked back to the Burglary Supervisor's office and stuck his head in. Said supervisor looked up, from his desk and asked "what can I do for you?"

The Detective answered with "I wanted to see if you had an air pump."

The supervisor, straining somewhat noticeably to not laugh, inquired "no but what do you need an air pump for anyway?"

The Detective, without skipping a beat, said "well, our secretary went out to her car, to go downtown for a paperwork run and all four tires on her care are flat."

One could almost see the color drain from the supervisor's face, as his eyes flitted from the right to the left and back again. He was clearly thinking and it was even more obvious that his conclusion was not good.

He said "all four tire huh? Uh, no, I don't have a pump. Good luck."

With that the Detective "circled" back around to the Narcotics Office and his waiting supervisor. Seconds later, they went totally unnoticed by the Burglary Detective, as the latter headed through the bay storage, with an air pump in hand.

At this point, both of the Narcotics guys went out the front door and carefully peered around the corner of the building, and watched as the tired were being filled with air.

Just as the last few pumps of air went into the final tire, the Narcotics Supervisor re-entered the building and walked out the side door he would normally use. He then walked up to his unit and seeing the Burglary Supervisor with the air pump still in-hand, opened his unit door with the key, got in and rolled his window down.

He looked at the Burglary Supervisor and said "man, I sure do appreciate your airing my tires up. I didn't know what I was going to do." With that, he drove off.

The Narcotics Detective, still watching, reported later that the Burglary Supervisor stood there for about a half-minute, at which time it fully hit him, as to how he had been conned. He threw the air pump and spat out some censorable expletives and walked back inside.

Things were never boring between those two Divisions.

25 | Oh Deer

Broadmoor Precinct, on Sharp Road in Baton Rouge, was almost literally a "hole in the wall" station that appeared as though it had been attached to the fire station there, as an afterthought. Regardless of how it came about, that little station produced a ton of memories and its share of memorable stories. Such was the case in 1981.

For those familiar with this particular station (it's been out of service for thirty plus years now), you really needed to know where it was in order to be able to locate it. It was in a residential area and not on what one would describe as a "main drag." I said that so you might understand a little better, the surprise two Officers felt, when, on dog shift, they exited the building at the same time two older ladies were driving up.

The real surprise was that these ladies were not from the Baton Rouge area. They were traveling from Texas to Florida and, according to what they told the Officers, had exited the interstate at Sherwood Forest Blvd., looking for gas. Now, remember, this was 1981 and Sherwood Forest Blvd., south of the interstate simply wasn't developed at that point.

In fact, at that time, there were still acres of woods on

both sides of the road and little to no traffic at 2 o'clock in the morning. The ladies to the Officers that they had exited I-12 and proceeded south on Sherwood Forest Blvd. Shortly after doing so, a deer had run out in front of their car and they hit it. Their primary concern was that the deer was suffering and wanted the Officers to "check it out."

Well, both Officers, being the diligent types they were, agreed wholeheartedly and headed to the location the ladies had described. Sure enough, there was indeed a deer. And as the Officers quickly noted, it wasn't suffering. The ladies had evidently hit it pretty solid as it was quite dead.

In 1981, as has been pointed out in earlier stories in this book, Officers were driving the small framed Chevrolet Malibu's, with the small 350 4-barrel under the hood. This translated into a relatively simple way to rid the roadway of the deer carcass. The Officers placed the doe on the hood of the unit and with their windows rolled down, one held onto the "ankles" while the driver held onto the "wrists" and off they went. Perhaps needless to say, the setup made for some unusual stares from the few stragglers that were out that late.

The Officers made it back to the Precinct with their "victim" and noted the ladies had departed. The shift Captain saw the doe lying on the hood and immediately instructed the Officers to "take care of it."

At this point, you may recall that it has been noted that Broadmoor Precinct was attached to a fire station. Well, behind this fire station was a hose tower, where the firefighters would suspend their hoses, after use, to clean and clear them out. At 2 o'clock in the morning this tower seemed perfectly suitable in which to clean a deer.

As the firefighters were fast asleep and the police radio was all but dead, it didn't take long to clean the deer and dispense of all the evidence. Well, almost all of the evidence.

6:00am arrived and the dog shift Officers were in the station, busily clearing out trip sheets and turning in reports. One of the two Officers, who had handled the "deer call" was up front, in the station, when the Fire Captain, from next door sauntered into the Precinct.

The Officer, surprised to see a firefighter that early, much less the station Captain, greeted him. "G'morning Captain, what's going on with you?"

The Captain, who incidentally, didn't arrive at that rank by being born just the day before, replied "I think you guys may want to call Homicide out."

The Officer, totally missing the mark, asked "why on earth would we want to call Homicide out?"

The Captain said "Judging by the amount of blood out there, I suspect there was a murder in our hose tower last night."

Well, the Officer, feeling just a tad sheepish at this point responded with "I don't really think there's a need to call Homicide out Captain. Do you boys like venison?"

The Captain grinned broadly and said "we most certainly do."

The Officers noted the trade-off was more than fair, as, in the dark, they had failed to see the accumulation of the deer blood and frankly, had failed to think about it. The fire Captain had said the venison looked so good that he "volunteered" a few of his men to go make the hose tower right. It's amazing how much water those fire hoses can push out in just a few minutes.

All-in-all, it was a good night. The deer call was handled and the two ladies, according to the Captain, had departed with high regards for the police in taking care of business. Both stations were well fed the next day and everyone was quite satisfied.

Some good times.

26 | The Jumper

1983, riding out of 2nd District on Highland Road in Baton Rouge, a Officer riding solo gets dispatched to the *Horace Wilkinson* bridge aka the "New Bridge" relative to a "jumper."

The Officer didn't get all crazy and turn the siren on; no, nothing like that. He just made his way to the bridge like anyone who may be out on a Sunday drive. And the reason for his not being in a hurry was the fact that this wasn't an unusual call.

A lot of folks don't realize it (some do and don't care), however, walking across the bridge is illegal. Does that stop anyone from doing so? Hardly. And typically, it's someone headed across the span to Port Allen that gets called in on as a "jumper." Other times, it's someone who breaks down or runs out of gas at the summit and then walks in seek of help.

This Officer had no reason to believe it would be anything other than one of the aforementioned scenarios, when he arrived at the bridge's peak and saw a lone individual standing on the top rail of the westbound lane. He quickly ignited his unit's rooftop bar lights and advised HQ, via radio, what he had.

Right here, let's back up just a little. Let's back up just a few days prior to this incident unfolding and note that this same Officer, while off-duty, had watched one of the latest Clint Eastwood *Dirty Harry* movies at home. Now, back to the bridge.

The Officer exits his unit, his eyes never leaving the guy on the railing. With his best imitation swagger combined with his most *laid back disinterested* voice he could muster, he addressed the troubled soul.

"Hey pardner, whatcha up to?" asked the Officer.

"Don't come any closer or I'll jump!!" yelled the man in response.

The Officer stopped in his tracks, inserted both thumbs behind his gunbelt, in a motion that would lead one to believe he was about to pull his pants up (the only thing missing was a toothpick in his mouth) and said "well, either jump or get down. I've got places to go and people......uh....crap!!"

The guy on the railing disappeared from view and the last motion the Officer saw was on the wrong side of the railing. As the Officer ran to the railing on which the man had been standing, he remembered thinking *this wasn't in the script!* Arriving at the railing, the Officer peered over at the mighty

Mississippi River, 175 feet below.

A few yards below the bottom rail and out of view of anyone standing, say, in the center of the bridge, was a piling. It was one of the original support pilings, from when the bridge was built and the main support beam protruded from the piling, leaving a significant ledge around the beam.

On this ledge, still very much alive, was the guy who had "jumped" (emphasized as he told Doctors later that he had slipped). He saw the Officer and yelled "I think my leg is broken, you gotta come down here and get me!"

Yeah, well, you just hold your breath on *that* happening. The Officer quickly contacted HQ and requested the Fire Department, informing them of the situation.

Before long, there were several more police units, Officers and supervisors as well as the Baton Rouge Fire Department being represented at the top of the bridge. Firefighters, trained in high-rise rescue techniques, used rappelling rope and gear to lower a firefighter and a basket to the ledge below.

Once the man was strapped into the basket, the other firefighter's topside began using a pulley system to pull the basket, containing the victim, up and over the top railing. Now, when the basket got to the top railing, the bottom of the basket was flush with the top of the rail, effectively standing the man up (he was strapped in) and at a slight angle. There were some twenty-five to thirty people, all standing on the northernmost lane on the westbound side. The guy in the basket points at one individual, which would be the initial Officer who was dispatched up there, and yelling at the top of his voice says "HE TOLD ME TO JUMP!!"

Several heads turn to look at the Officer who responds with "well, I guess that's pretty clear. He's a NUT!"

The guy who jumped was treated for a broken ankle and placed under psychiatric observation for a time. He ended up coming out better than when he went in.

The Officer worked on some new verbal techniques, just in case the need should arise again; however, that was his first and last jumper, ever, in his entire career.

Everything's good if *everyone* follows the script.

27 | Uh, Officer

We're going to pull another story, for you, from the Rescue Division files. It's 1984 and the location is the northbound lane of Airline Hwy. under the I-12 overpass.

There has been an auto accident at this location and moderate, non-life-threatening injuries are reported. For the sake of explaining how this takes place, one must know that there is a "new guy" in Rescue and the new guy has recently graduated a class, which certifies him as an official EMT (Emergency Medical Technician).

There's little, in the known world that is more eager to practice that which they have just learned, than a law enforcement officer who has been certified in something. It doesn't really matter what they have been certified in, however, the more recent the certification, the more eager they are to display that expertise.

Such was the case on this day in 1984. The new guy responds to the scene of the wreck. As luck would have it, he beats the ambulance to the scene. The only one there ahead of him, is the primary uniform officer, who is writing the accident.

The new guy drives up in one of the Rescue Divisions Ford Broncos. From his vantage point, the new guy observes a female lying on her back, in the middle of the right lane on the northbound side. He promptly exits the unit and grabs the orange-colored first-responder kit, containing everything he could possibly need and most everything he doesn't need.

He makes a beeline for the stricken lady, who, incidentally, is fully conscious and cognizant of her situation. The newly certified EMT makes a rather fast diagnosis and determines his next action, prior to actually treating the vict--..., er, patient. Thus far, no verbal exchange between our hero and the accident victim.

Our non-caped crusader opens the triage kit and removes.....he removes....scissors? The then, quite expertly I might add, begins cutting the young woman's pants and removing them. It was approximately halfway through the first leg, when the victim (now she's very much a victim), speaks out.

"Uh, Officer."

Our hero replies "be with you in a minute ma'am, just relax, I'll take care of you."

"But Officer....."

"It's okay ma'am, I know what I'm doing."

"Well, that's good to know Officer; would you happen to know that it's my arm that was hurt in the wreck and not either of my legs?" she asked ever so sweetly.

By this time, one entire pants leg had been removed and EMS was arriving on the scene. The EMS Paramedics walk up and as one might surmise, assume that the victims' leg is injured, albeit an "invisible" injury. They look at the Officer, when the victim says "it's my arm that's hurt, I promise you."

Our eager, would-be hero surrenders the victim over to the Paramedics and then quietly gathers his equipment and heads for the unit. Without a word, he leaves the scene.

One of the first things that has been taught, over the years, in the Baton Rouge Police Academy is one should never *assume* anything, as doing so, can make an ....

ass • u • me

In this case, the only ass learned a hard lesson.

28 | I Need EMS Code 3

It's 1984 in the First District area, in Baton Rouge.

A solo uniform patrol Officer drives upon an MVA (Motor Vehicle Accident) at the intersection of Plank Rd. and Hollywood. A motorcycle is involved and by all appearances, the accident is serious.

The Officer, still moving and peering from his driver's side window sees the operator of the motorcycle lying prone on the pavement. A few feet away from the rider is one of his legs, the latter no longer attached to his torso.

"HQ, send me EMS code 3 (red lights & siren)" screamed the Officer into his microphone. He added "tell'em the driver has lost his leg!"

The Officer exits his unit and approaches the hapless rider, who is still wearing his helmet. "Son, just try and relax, I have an ambulance coming for you."

The young motorcycle rider props himself up onto his

elbows, look at the Officer and says "thank but if you'll just give me my prosthesis, I don't think I'll need an ambulance. I can't walk without it."

Sometimes the simplest things can be overlooked, even when they are right under your nose.

29 | Lagniappe

I thought I would close out this book of stories with some down-home, south Louisiana lagniappe (a little something extra).

Law enforcement officers through the ages have all, in one form or another, run across that person who "pays their salary" or is "a good friend and supporter of the Mayor" or is "the Police Chief's 3rd cousin from a previous marriage." In other words, at one time or another, provided one stays with the job long enough, we have all run across that "special butthead" whose sole mission in life, so it appears, is to make a cops life miserable.

After several years of doing this job, one tends to develop his or her own collection of "canned responses." That is, responses that come rolling off the tongue, easily, with little to no effort in thinking about it.

I thought, as an added bonus, I would share with you, some of the best responses I've heard (and used) over the years.

1. "You know, stop lights don't come any redder than the

one you just went through."

2. "Relax, the handcuffs are tight because they're new. They'll stretch after you wear them a while."

3. "If you take your hands off the car, I'll make your birth certificate a worthless document."

4. "If you run, you'll only go to jail tired."

5. "Can you run faster than 1200 feet per second? Because that's the speed of the bullet that will be chasing you."

6. "You don't know how fast you were going? I guess that means I can write anything I want to on the ticket, huh?"

7. "Yes, sir, you can talk to the shift supervisor, but I don't think it will help. Oh, did I mention that I'm the shift supervisor?"

8. "Warning! You want a warning? O.K, I'm warning you not to do that again or I'll give you another ticket."

9. "The answer to this last question will determine whether you are drunk or not. Was Mickey Mouse a cat or a dog?"

10. "Fair? You want me to be fair? Listen, fair is a place where you go to ride on rides, eat cotton candy and corn dogs and step in monkey poop."

11. "Yeah, we have a quota. Two more tickets and my wife gets a toaster oven."

12. "In God we trust; all others we run through NCIC." (National Crime Information Center)

13. "Just how big were those 'two beers' you say you had?"

14. "No sir, we don't have quotas anymore. We used to, but now we're allowed to write as many tickets as we can."

15. "I'm glad to hear that the Chief (of Police) is a personal friend of yours. So you know someone who can post your bail."

16. "You didn't think we give pretty women tickets? You're right, we don't. Sign here."

Acknowledgements

This section of the book is short, relatively speaking, largely due to the fact that the characters that made the stories are anonymous. Nonetheless, I know most of them, personally and truly thank them for the many wonderful memories and laughs they and their actions generated.

With that said, I feel compelled to name a few folks whose contributions, with their time and memories, have served to add some of the chapters you've read.

First in my life is Jesus Christ. Suffice it to say, that without Him, period, this book, nothing, would be possible. He gave me a love for reading and writing and an ability to do both. I truly hope and pray that He would use this book to Glorify His Name and Kingdom.

I thank my lovely better-half, Teri, for putting up with me and the deadline in which I had to meet to get this book out. I would "disappear" for hours at a time, to focus on writing and wrestle with what stories should be considered and which should be put aside. She encouraged me through it all.

There are some people, which you just naturally like when you first meet them. Sometimes, the friendship that is developed endures. Such is the case with one particular contributor to this book, with whom I am truly blessed to have called a friend for almost forty years.

Brett Smith and I first met when we worked together at the East Baton Rouge Parish Sheriff's Office in 1978. We became friends and in 1980, he followed me to the Baton Rouge Police Department, entering the 44th BTA (Basic Training Academy), one class behind me.

We ended up as riding partners in 1981 and the friendship that already existed simply grew stronger. It has never waned. So, when I got in touch with Brett, regarding this book, there wasn't a moment's hesitation. He read, contributed, suggested and ultimately approved of everything I sent his way.

With his permission, I must tell you that this book would be sorely lacking (read: not exist) without the roles he played in some of the stories. I'll leave it at that. I truly appreciate the support and encouragement. Even more, I appreciate the friendship.

Then, in the 1990's I was assigned to a squad out of Second District on Highland Road. The squad was a virtual smorgasbord of characters, who worked well together. I ended up teaming up with one character in particular and who also became a contributor to this book as well; Tommy Dewey.

Most of what I could write about the days Tommy and I served together in Uniform Patrol would prove of better service in classroom settings, however, one in particular had to be recorded for the sake of posterity. And so it has been. Having served over three decades in law enforcement, prior to retiring, Tommy Dewey contributed to the single funniest event I ever had the enjoyment of witnessing. Read that again. The "hint" is there, as to which story I'm referring to.

Tommy retired from the department after twenty years and is now a successful attorney in Baton Rouge. I feel fortunate to still call him a friend as well. Thanks for the memories Brother. I still enjoy a hearty laugh when I recall that evening.

Finally, I want to thank someone from my long ago past. Someone, when I name her, most will say "who?" The reason for the unfamiliarity is that she wasn't from the Baton Rouge area, where this book gets its foundation and walls from.

Thank you, Mrs. Mabel Sessions.

Mrs. Sessions was my 7th-grade teacher in Urania, Louisiana. I remember Mrs. Sessions as being a very prim and proper lady, who absolutely loved LSU sports, especially anything involving her "hero" at the time, "Pistol Pete"

Maravich. That class knew who Pete Maravich was, as we received an almost daily update on his record-setting skills on the basketball court.

I also remember Mrs. Sessions for one other instance; one that ended up having a profound impact on how I view and approach writing, to this very day.

One morning, Mrs. Sessions directed her class to "write a story." The story she said, could be on anything, personal, fiction, pets, it didn't matter. The only requirement was that the story be 100% original, non-plagiarized. Each student would read their own story, out-loud, to her and the rest of the class.

The day came and I listened intently to the stories others ahead of me had penned. Then my turn came. I began reading a story I made up about WWII and the crew of a B-17 bomber (I knew enough to use my encyclopedia's for research) that barely made it back to base after a mission. The story was 100% original on my part and the few errors that I did make in its creation further assured Mrs. Sessions of that fact.

At the end of the reading, Mrs. Sessions looked at me and said "you would do well if you follow writing for a career and study accordingly."

Mrs. Sessions, of course, had no way of knowing, at the

time, how her accolade affected me that day. I was more proud of what she said to me in open class than of any other time throughout the years I spent in school. I never forgot it or her.

R. I. P. Mrs. Sessions. I thank you for the encouragement, which meant more to me than you could ever know.

About the Author

Ron served with the East Baton Rouge Parish Sheriff's Office from 1978 – 1980.

In 1980, Ron entered the 43rd Basic Training Academy for the Baton Rouge Police Department. During his career there, Ron served in Uniform Patrol, Rescue, Narcotics and Homicide/Robbery. He also served as Commander of Computer Operations, Mobile Data, Crime Information Unit and the Crime Analysis Unit.

He retired in 2011 as Commander of 4th District, at the rank of Captain.

The author can always be reached at his website.

http://www.RonCowart.com/

Made in the USA
Middletown, DE
06 June 2021

41289155R00076